10/21

With Thanks for your work supporting Chicago arts and culture,

Julie Parson-Nesbitt
_3/15/00_

A DECADE OF POETRY FROM CHICAGO'S GUILD COMPLEX

POWER LINES

EDITED BY

JULIE PARSON-NESBITT

LUIS J. RODRIGUEZ

AND MICHAEL WARR

D1472022

TIA CHUCHA PRESS
CHICAGO

Printed in the United States of America

ISBN 1-882699-22-8

Library of Congress Catalog Card Number: 99-72837

Book Design: Jane Brunette
Cover Painting: "Back of the Yards" by Tony Fitzpatrick

Published by:
Tia Chucha Press
A Project of the Guild Complex
PO Box 476969
Chicago IL 60647

Distributed by:
Northwestern University Press
Chicago Distribution Center
11030 South Langley Avenue
Chicago IL 60628

Tia Chucha Press and the Guild Complex have received support from the John D. and Catherine
T. MacArthur Foundation, Lannan Foundation, Sara Lee Foundation, National Endowment for
the Arts, the Illinois Arts Council, Kraft Foods, City of Chicago Department of Cultural Affairs,
Lila Wallace-Readers Digest Fund, Eric Mathieu King Fund of the Academy of American Poets,
The Chicago Community Foundation, the Reva and David Logan Foundation, the Illinois
Humanities Council, Poets & Writers, The Woods Fund of Chicago, WPWR-TV Channel 50
Foundation, The Mayer & Morris Kaplan Family Foundation, Driehaus Foundation, and the
Elizabeth F. Cheney Foundation.

ACKNOWLEDGMENTS

The blood, sweat, and tears of the following people went into this project: Jane Haldiman, who during her internship at the Guild Complex proved that God is in the details, Jen Abrams, Emily Banner, Kerstin Broockmann, Maneolla Gonzalez, Jane Brunette, Tony Fitzpatrick, Rohan Preston for the poem that gave us the title *Power Lines*, Mark Ingebretsen, Reginald Gibbons, Quraysh Ali Lansana, Leslie Schict, Lynn Bulgrin, Katherine Stewart, Dena Roberts, and Jennifer Ambrose.

Grateful acknowledgment is made for the following poems:

"Two Dedications, I. The Chicago Picasso and II. The Wall." From *Blacks* by Gwendolyn Brooks, Third World Press, 1992. Reprinted by permission of the author.

"For My Child Who Became a Man on His Thirteenth Year." From the forthcoming *I Ask The Impossible*. Copyright © 1998 by Ana Castillo. To be published in English. Reprinted by permission of Susan Bergholz Literary Services, New York. All rights reserved.

"Cloud." From *Loose Woman*. Copyright © 1994 by Sandra Cisneros. Published by Vintage Books, a division of Random House, Inc., and originally in hardcover by Alfred A. Knopf, Inc. Reprinted by permission of Susan Bergholz Literary Services, New York. All rights reserved.

"After A Reading At A Black College." From *Tender* by Toi Derricotte, University of Pittsburgh Press. Reprinted by permission of the author.

"From 'A,' the End of the Earth." From *Swimmer's Prayer* by Cynthia Gallagher, Missing Spoke Press, 1999. Reprinted by permission of the author.

"Canticus Narcissus" by Paul Hoover was published in *American Poetry Review*, 1999. Reprinted by permission of the publisher.

"Fin-de-Siècle Blues" by Carolyn Kizer. From *American Poets Say Goodbye to the 20th Century*, edited by André Codrescu, 4 Walls/8 Windows, 1996. Reprinted by permission of the author.

"Mistress of Nothing" by Olivia Maciel. From *Shards of Light/Astillas De Luz*, Tia Chucha Press, 1998. Reprinted by permission of the publisher.

"Halcyon Days" by Lisel Mueller was published in *Chelsea #64*, 40th Anniversary Issue, 1998. Reprinted by permission of the author.

"Family values" by Marge Piercy was published in *Caprice*, August 1998. Reprinted by permission of the author.

"Roses" by Deborah Pintonelli was published in *Ego Monkey*, ACP 1991. Reprinted by permission of the author.

"Fighting Fire" is from *Walking Back Up Depot Street* by Minnie Bruce Pratt, © 1999. Reprinted by permission of the University of Pittsburgh Press.

"Gray Day in January in La Jolla: 1997 For Porter Sylvanus Troupe." From *Choruses* by Quincy Troupe, Coffee House Press, 1999. Reprinted by permission of the author.

T A B L E O F

C O N T E N T S

INTRODUCTION

THE FEDERAL AGENT pulled his badge out of a leather flack jacket and growled the words "welcome to the real world." But it was a poetry bash, not a crack party. It was not a drug dealer he was menacing, but a Guild Complex volunteer taking admissions at our Eighth National Poetry Video Festival. We were being busted, at least according to the Ramboesque agent, "for charging admissions without a license." He didn't have a legal leg to stand on, but still the cash box was confiscated and entry to the event blocked. Police raided the two floors of events, shutting down the poetry video slam and "make your own poetry video" studio. Audience members were forced to vacate the building. Downstairs, the volunteer and I were detained in a sweltering squad car with the windows and doors locked so we could not escape. This really happened. We have it on video.

After initial disbelief, followed by a maddening mix of shouting, posturing, pleading, maneuvering, and negotiating, the District Commander eventually told Rambo he had to let us go. As I sat in the squad car and watched the crowd pour out of the building under order of the police, I thought how Keystonian these officers must feel. This had to be like no bust they had ever made. However, it was a made-for-movie reflection of a Guild Complex crowd. There were parents with kids, urbanites, suburbanites, hip-hop crews, teachers and students, techheads, people of every age, color, and ethnic group, and of course poets and artists, not to mention the featured German artists and technicians, who had flown all the way from Europe to experience this Orwellian spectacle.

Of course the poetry went on. As always.

At the Complex, we rejoice in mixing and shaking things up. Whether it is a night of Adrienne Rich and Patricia Smith, the sonnets of Shakespeare with the soulful voice of poet Angela Jackson, dance improvisation to poetry, the solo voice of Li-Young Lee, or the poems of Rumi behind percussion, each event establishes a link based in human experience and voice.

There is a story waiting to be told about contemporary poetry in Chicago, its creative dissemination, and its impact on the state of poetry in North America. Through the blending of the voices of poets from Chicago and across the nation who have been featured at the Guild Complex, *Power Lines: A Decade of Poetry From Chicago's Guild*

Complex tells part of that saga.

Sitting at a café writing this introduction, I watched as two customers were drawn to the inevitable billboard of announcements. A Guild Complex poster featuring poet Joy Harjo caught their eye. One of them began to sing her praises. I walked over to them, pulled out copies of the Complex calendar from under a pile and handed one to each of them. Turned out one of them had just moved back to Chicago and was amazed at the new range of literary happenings. Things were not always this way. It may be common now to see poetry events and venues that regularly include writers from Chicago's diverse neighborhoods, featuring the spectrum of poetic forms, but even ten years ago such diversity was still an anomaly. At the Complex it was the norm. We inherited the attitude and action of cross-cultural programming from our parent organization, Guild Books, which was known internationally for its sections on African-American, Latin-American, Asian-American, Labor and Women's Studies, long before such sections became a feature at chain bookstores.

The Complex, however, also emerged out of a political climate that was conducive to its mission of providing a forum for literary cross-cultural expression. As that mission was being formed, communities in Chicago were immersed in the popular campaign to elect Chicago's first African-American Mayor, Harold Washington, who was an avid reader and a regular customer at Guild Books. At the time, the Washington Campaign was a rare symbol of diversity in practice in Chicago, as was Guild Books. Diversity, like politics, is in our blood.

But Chicago was also divided and all was not peace and love. Even the appearance of a literary star could be dangerous. When James Baldwin appeared at Guild Books, a group of neo-nazis threatened the novelist's life and the bookstore. Rising to the occasion, poet and painter Tony Fitzpatrick mobilized a burly crew to protect Mr. Baldwin. I still have that image of the former-boxer-turned-artist standing outside the store in a beret ready to break a few fascist bones. A sensationalist headline could have read "Irish-American Poet/Painter/Boxer Protects Gay African-American Literary Icon from Fascists at Guild Books Reading," but it was just a day in the life of Guild.

I am proud of our instinctive gravitation toward the synthesis of art forms, mediums, and cultures, which is equally as strong as our pull toward distinctive representation. While we were supportive of Chicago cultural institutions such as Spices, an African American-centered poetry series that may be best known for inspiring the film "lovejones," and MARCH/Abrazo Press, which focuses on Latino literature, it was also through our central participation in such events as the Printer's Row Book Fair and the Neutral Turf Poetry Festival — born as a means to unite the splintered poetry community and as a fundraiser for Guild Books — that we contributed to the evolution of Chicago's literary scene into a more diverse community than it has ever been.

Our ability, or maybe even our need, to mix it up in a city known internationally for segregation is probably what makes the heart of the Complex beat. It was born diverse and would die if it tried to be something else.

As a child of Guild Books — where poetry performances and books coexisted— we were never caught up in an artificial conflict between page and stage. "Performance poets" and "academic poets" converged upon the same book section at the store. The people sitting around the table at the Red Lion Pub to conceptualize and create the Complex were all influenced by literature and art and a desire to change the world. At the table were Vicki Capalbo, Mitch "Mitar" Covic, David Hernandez, Reginald Gibbons, Julie Parson-Nesbitt, Luis Rodríguez, Lew Rosenbaum, Nancy Singham, Sue Ying and myself. And in spirit from the West Coast, Richard Bray. It was a natural part of our evolution, that Tia Chucha Press, founded by poet, writer and publisher Luis Rodríguez, my roommate at the time, would eventually become the publishing wing of the Guild Complex.

All of this happened in the context of a poetry movement that was national and international. Poetry Slams, born in Chicago, were reawakening parts of the poetry world that had lain dormant. The Slam offered a vibrant, democratic, popular environment that created new poets and new audiences. One pundit wrote that poetry had died; in fact it was in the process of resurrection. New forms were emerging and shoving their way in beside old forms. The revitalization of popular interest in poetry, even when controversial, led to an expanded interest in all things poetic — whether the form resided behind ivy walls, in cinema houses, psychiatric wards, cafes, bars, board rooms, or magnetically attached to people's refrigerators.

The resurgence of poetry is not due only to Slam poetry. Hip Hop has provided a catalyst for a new generation of poets, raising the always pivotal role of the poet in the African-American and Latino communities to another level. Teachers, seeing the ability of poetry to pull students into reading and writing, are demanding poets in the schools and creating a new generation of poetry-literate youth. Artists have gained unprecedented access to new technologies that facilitate the merging of poetry with film, video, digital and new-media technology. With the revolutionization of computer technology, poets are armed with their own presses, websites, email, MP3 technology, and other forms of digital distribution to add to the idea arsenal. We are empowered by the tools and technologies that enable us to spread poetry by any means necessary.

The power of poetry comes from our ability to create a poem, or to be engulfed in its creation, even if we are propertyless and penniless. Poetry is not owned. For many, poetry sheds light as well as art. If necessary or desired, poetry can be created without pen, pencil, or computer, which means no one can take the ability to create away from the poet. Poetry does not wait for decree or demand. As long as there is a search for a primal link to people, for solutions to social equations, and for that way of saying what can not be said in ordinary language, poetry will remain the people's means of expression.

Power Lines: A Decade of Poetry From Chicago's Guild Complex is a means of achieving on the page what the Complex does every week on stage: offer poetry that matters, in a challenging array of voices. In these pages are poets who pound words with jackhammers, alongside poets who hold words between their fingers as if delicately threading a needle. Pulitzer Prize-winning poets are juxtaposed with poets being published for the first time in this anthology. Performance poets share these pages with poets who perform only in front of a lectern. And in *Power Lines*, as on the Guild Complex stage, Chicago poets appear with poets from across the country and the world. What the poets in this anthology share is their ability to get under your skin and inside your soul with their words.

Michael Warr, Chicago, September 1999

My Neighbors

My neighbors are a clan of serene barbarians whose sole purpose it
seems, exist in disturbing the peacefulness of my tiny sanctuary,
hidden between city concretes and atmospheric black holes.

This sanctuary filled with ancient bibliographies and fine tawny port
from Oporto.

Here spirits dwell in divine lechery and there are those coming
to worship, in effect have called them here.

But every night about three a.m. the barbarians enter with
obstreperous feet.
Boom!...here comes one now. Listen! As they proceed to move every
piece of their barbarian furniture across the floor.

Boomclankblo!... Now this will be their barbarous music, they'll go on
like this for two hours or more as I contemplate the virtues of
government and the in-virtues of impatience.

Which of them shall I assassinate first!!

But alas!... how I've lost the will to suppress stupidity... bump off
belligerence.

So I meditate on neither this nor that
and on the soul in everything.

I ring up the wizards to join me for a twilight mocha java latte.
Pop in a CD of esoteric chanting and the barbarians now flaccid and
befuddled by bata drums and my Bakongo dissolve into the
underground for three to six weeks until another sprouting.

Later I work on my character.

The Sun King (1974)

James Hampton, the Sun King
of Washington, DC
erects a tin-foil throne.
"Where there is no vision, the people perish."
Altar, pulpit, light-bulbs.

My 14th and "U," my 34 bus, my weekday winos,
my white-robed black Israelites
on their redstone stoops,
my graffiti: "Anna the Leo as 'Ice,'"
my neon James Brown poster
coming to the DC Coliseum
where all I will see is the circus,
my one visit to RKO Keith's Theater
to see "Car Wash"
and a bird flew in, and mania,
frantic black shadow on the screen,
I was out of the house in a theater full of black folks,
black people, black movie, black bird,
I was out, I was free, I was at RKO Keith's Theater
at 14th and "U"
and it was not "Car Wash" it was the first
Richard Pryor concert movie
and a bird flew in the screen
and memory is romance
and race is romance,
and the Sun King lives
in Washington, DC.

Three Winter Songs

"a cupful of syllables"
—Angela Jackson

I.
silence and its attendant
    particles, lint spun
        along the windowshade's

bright fissure, morning
    light, the kitchen's moist air
        quavering, crazed radiator,

windowsill, pale velvet,
    untended, brittle African
        violet leaves, hands, fingertips,

syllables paced out,
    one breath at a time, against
        the table edge do sway, do dance

II.
City! if love is a circle
    and morning is its radius,
        can night be its center

or the darkness that
    surrounds it played at
        or among, as though

it were shaped into
    treeforms and gangways,
        spaces your breath recalls

or footsteps strike
    as you go quickly,
        the passing contours

of bark and brickwork,
　　yours by right of
　　　　unprovoked remembering?

whose body is this
　　anyway, leaning, whose spirit
　　　　lifts your arms now,

your voice soft
　　and unexpected? child's
　　　　play, these unlit presences,

pasts traced in sooted
　　snow, bits of bright glass
　　　　held beneath darkened ice,

the way home, the way
　　back, alley after alley,
　　　　street names rung out;

center, of course, and perimeter
　　bent inward with your
　　　　fingers, and what is held there

and said once again,
　　a song, nouns reeling to
　　　　their own sweet whisperings

III.
do sway, do dance —
　　fingertips, fingernails
　　　　busy with words,

a song does leaf here,
　　and what you say now
　　　　says its flowering, is made

of light and water, snow-
　　quick and greening, petalled,
　　　　the sepalling syllables

say street, say lamppost,
　　brickbat, what was scrawled
　　　　red in gray concrete, called out,

arms asway and bare shoulders
　　counting the music, summer, all
　　　　that the snow's pale present

covers, layers in and slows
　　rises in your throat and flares
　　　　across the window's chill panes

Better Than The Movies

It was
a summer afternoon
and it was
the sun
that lit our view
and it was
a day to spend
with friends.

And there was
sun light
camera eyes
and action
from a hand gun.

And it was
at the corner store
and he laid
on the cement floor
and it was
the neighbors
that gathered to see
he   that   was
fourteen.

And it was
his cheek
stuck on the street
and he had
three bullets
in his back
and he was alone
with no mother
to cry good-bye.

And it was
the police that came
and it was
one cop that smiled
and said,
"This is better
        than the movies."

The Writer At Her Work

Her work is never done. It brings out
dirt and dust; it makes water
marks and holes. Her work is clay pots
and straw baskets, drawers, hidden
compartments. Her work is letters
secretly read under the streetlamp. Her work
is greasy and raw, made of wings and blood
and screams. Her work is a tooth, a tongue,
a bone. A lump of sugar, a maze, a silk thread — white
and bright. Her work is never done.

A tongue sucking a tooth, her work
is dangerous, slippery, foreign. Her work
is painful and pained, hurtful and hurt. Continents
cannot contain it. It overflows, spills from
the sides, oozes sticky and yellow
from each crevice left open,
uncovered. Her work is never done.

The edges yawn, let out steam, vapor,
smells. The edges curl up and away. Her work
soothes, rages, and sweats. Her work is
inside her body. It comes out
from moist interstices, creeping, snaking its way
towards the others. Her work is never done.

She will work until her last breath, her final sigh.

Traveling Black
New Mexico 1991, Europe 1992

Traveling black in New Mexico,
you wonder how you fit the local
color scheme. One of just ten blacks you've seen,
are your loyalties with the native Americans,

Nuevo Mexicanos or *turistas*?
You've paid ten bucks admission
and five to bring your camera, and now stand
in the Taos Pueblo parking lot, not knowing
if you'll join the California/Texans eager
for a "squaw"-guided tour,

peeking and peering in forbidden windows,
warned against clicking without permission and a tip,
but still gawking like patrons in a zoo
at workers patching a roof, and chuckling
at the four-year-old perched on an adobe sill
who threatens to cut off white noses
with his pre-school scissors.

Traveling black, you wonder how they'd feel
if a busload of redfolk showed up in their subdivision
and started sketching hieroglyphs of
bathrobed middle-managers taking in the paper
and mighty braves from Sears
installing aluminum siding.

So you stand by the pueblo stream,
equidistant from white man and red,
snapping the beehive buildings from afar
to steal nobody's dignity,
then go back to your car.

Traveling black in Paris, you wonder if they
really love black artists more than they hate

Algerians, who, like the Vietnamese,
kicked Jules *et* Jacques off their continents.
Just stride through the Arc de Triomphe and declare,
"Je suis un poète Americain,
le fils de Josephine Baker et Richard Wright"
and they'll give you the keys to the city?
Or is that a myth, like in the States
the streets are paved with gold?

Traveling black in Paris, you wait in Gare de l'Est
and watch commuters dash from trains,
les hommes et les femmes d'affaires,
white, black, desert-brown and far-east fair,
and you think how it's a civilized New York
with nobody at anybody's throat,

and note that the French women aren't afraid
to share a block with two black tourists
wandering the Quarter *ce soir, à vingt-trois heures.*
Traveling black in Paris, you try to guess
which blacks are yours and which are theirs,
if Africans will give you the standard
nod-*de-frère*, or if they're too proud of their full blood

to acknowledge brothers in jeans and sneakers
who *parler* not enough *Français*
to pass for Senegalese.

Traveling black into Frankfurt's airport,
the halls are filled with young Colin Powells
being all they can be, who serve what's left of NATO
by stitching with their wrenches the black bellies
of B-52s we taxied past on landing.

Traveling black on downtown streets
in Frankfurt, under gleaming giant logos
of microchip multi-nationals in the high-tech Reich,
past an ancient cathedral and an endless sex-show strip,
you wonder if those two are just Americans
with jerry-curls, or from Ethiopia or Sudan
or someplace else where negroes have good hair.

But, traveling black in Berlin,
you see no one like you on Kuferstendam,
the main street of the west. In the east,
you look for swastikas on the run-down buildings,
warned ten times upon leaving the States
that skinheads here skin Turks
and won't love your black ass, either.

Ja, traveling black in Germany,
you'd rather say, *"Ich bin ein Frankfurter,"*
a city flooded with foreign faces and capital,
than *"ein Berliner,"* where you're a novelty,
where doilies in a café are printed with pickaninnies,
where Levi's actually dares market a line
of hip-hop clothes called Black Culture™.

Traveling black in Berlin, you're cheered
to note that where "nazi" is displayed,
it's *"Nazi Raus!"* the anti-racists are spraying.
But you don't know what to make
of the only sister you meet,
already soused at noon in a working-class bar —
army brat abandoned in the land of Hans and Franz? —
She waits an hour, then comes over
and in weak English says that
"you are black like me, *ja?* In Germany,
deutschmarks are everything,
you have them, you're on top,
you don't, you're less than nothing,
there's the high and the low, but no — how you say it? —
middle; *ja, ja,* fuck Germany, it's all about *marks,"*
and she knows she drinks too much,
but she doesn't tell you if what she repeats
like a bitter mantra is why: *"Ja, ja,*
fuck Germany, fuck Germany."

In Town

Something in the way of things
Something that will quit and wont start
Something you know but cant stand cant know
But get along with. Like Death riding on top of the car
Peering through the windshield for
His cue Something entirely fictitious
And true, that creeps across your path
Halloing your evil ways, like they were
Yourself passing yourself not smiling

The dead guy you saw me talking to
Is your boss, I tried to put a spell
On him, but his spirit is illiterate
I know things you know, and nothing
You don't know. Except I saw something
In the way of things, something grinning
At me, And I wanted to know, was it funny
Was it so funny, it followed me down the street
Greeting everybody like the Good Humor Man
And they got the taste of the Good Humor, but no Ice
Cream. It was like that. Me talking across people
Into houses, and not seeing the beings crowding
Around me with ice picks. You cd see them, but they looked
Like important negroes on the way to your funeral. They looked
Like important jigaboos on the way to your auction. They let
Them chant the numbers and use an ivory pointer
To count your teeth. Remember Step n Fechit, How we laughed
Knowing it was Sunday School images given flesh and jiggling
With the Ice pick high over his head, made you laugh anyway.

I can see something in the way of ourselves
That's why I say the things I do. You know it
But it's something else to you. Like that job,
This morning, when you got there, it was quiet
And the machines were yearning soft behind you
Yearning for their nigger to come and give up his life
Standing there being dissed and broke and troubled.

My mistake is I kept saying that was proof God didn't exist.
And you told me Naw, it was proof that the Devil DO.
But still its like I see something, I hear things, I saw words
    In the white boys lying rag said you was gonna die poor
        and frustrated
That them dreams walk with you cross town, is gonna die
        from overwork
That the garbage on the street is telling you you aint shit and you
        almost believe it
Broke and mistaken all the time. You know some of the words.
        But they aint
The right ones. Your cable back on, but aint nothing on it you can see
But I see something in the way of things. Something make us stumble.
Something get us drunk from noise and addicted to sadness. I see
        something
And feel something stalking us, Like a ugly thing floating at our back
Calling us names. You see it, and hear it too, but you say it gotta right
To exist, just like you. And if God made it, but then we got to argue
And the light gon' come down around us. Even though we remember
Where the bank is. Remember the negro squinting at us through
        the cage.

You seen what I see too. A smile that aint a smile but teeth flying
        against our necks
You see something too, but cant call its name. Aint it too bad, yall
        said, Aint it too
Bad. Such a nice boy. Always kind to his mother. Always say good
        morning to
everybody, on his way to work. But that last time before he got locked
        up and hurt
Real bad. I seen him walking toward his house and he wasn't smiling
        and he didn't
Even say Hello. But I knew he'd seen something. Something in the
        way of things.
And it worked on him, like it do and will. And he kept marching
        faster and faster
Away from us, and never even muttered a word. Then the next day,
        he was gone!

You wanna know what...what I'm talking about. Sayin, I seen
        something

something

In the way of things. And how the boy's face looked that day, just before they took

him away. There is in that face, and remember, now, remember all them other faces

And all the many places you seen him or the sister with his child wandering up the

street. Remember what you seen in your own mirror, and didn't for a second

Recognize the face, your own face, straining to get out from behind the glass.

Open your mouth like you was gonna say something. Close your eyes and remember

What you saw, and what it made you feel like. Now don't you see something else,

Something cold and ugly, not invisible but blended with the shadow criss-crossing

The old man squatting by the drug store at the corner with his head resting uneasily

On his folded arms. And the boy that smiled. And the girl he went with, and in my

eyes too, a waving craziness splitting them into the jet stream of a black bird

His ass on fire, or the solemn notness of where we go to know we gon' be happy.

I seen something and you seen it too. You just cant call its name.

Night Crawl

My second night on Okinawa,
I slept out on the beach with a Spec 5 named Frenchy.
I remember waking up and looking out over the China Sea,
Dark and flat as smoked glass,
With only the finest serration at the sides of the moon's runway
To break the illusion of mirror.
The moon was almost full,
Throwing, from horizon to shore, an iridescent path
So straight and so solid,
I could have marched across the deserted shadowless sand,
Danced up the glimmering pavement, and peered over the edge
In less time than it takes to say, "Follow the Platinum Road."
Yes, I *knew*. At that very moment, I *knew*.
(Even as an irreverent thought grazed the back of my mind like a
    stray bullet,
"This is what it looks like just before Godzilla appears!")
I *knew* — I was aware that never again, as long as I lived,
Would I be in this place again,
Seeing what I was seeing.

Tonight we're driving back into the city,
After doing a show somewhere in the north suburbs.
Your other passenger decided to ride home with the band,
So we're alone in the car.
It's rained earlier, but the stars are twinkling out,
Making more stars out of the raindrops scattered
    on the green blackness
And the fragments of white metal sprinkled over my stage clothes.
There's no moon but the headlights,
And the only reflection is the line down the center of the highway.
Nothing moves tonight but us.

"Mary," you ask, your voice high and uncertain at the wheel,
"Do you think the next generation is less fucked up than we are?"
"Yeah—*yeah*, I think so." I reply,
Glad when you don't ask me *why* I think so.

Smitty, this little gray Buick is too much like a bunker,
And the shadows out there too much like a jungle,
And this night too still and silent
To risk talking, making the noises,
Awakening those thousands of terrifying creatures
Hiding in the darkness, too small to be seen by starlight,
Who will remind us that we will never be here again.

At The Stove

I.
Twining her fingers around the spokes,
she drags the blue chair across the kitchen.
Climbing, she plants bare feet.
Her ankles swivel. Her arms float
at her sides like wings.

Bending close to the mother,
she reaches for the wooden spoon.
Darting, her hand quivers.
The blue chair wobbles.
The mother goes on stirring the soup.

II.
It is a moment when
the course of a universe may be decided,
the spoon retained or relinquished,
the language spoken — that of
humiliation or praise.

It is a question of
whether the mother, apprehending the moment,
can imagine the child as woman
in some distant kitchen
in some distant place.

III.
Imagine the mother wrapping her own hand
around the child's like a cape.
The first wild stirring.
The chair rocking
as if beset by waves.

Imagine the calm as the mother's touch prevails.
The ripple that passes like satin

along the child's coiled spine.
The chair coming to rest
on the weathered floorboards.

The shining flowers of her feet.

Poem For Wicker Park Yuppies
(A True Story)

You people
talk about travesties, Eurodollar exchange rates
        in a foreign land
        I can't find on a map
'cuz I went to Chicago public schools
& maybe 'cuz I barely been out of the neighborhood still

You know what's happening all around the world
but you don't know what's going on all in front of your face

Hey! I said you people so well informed
reading the paper all morning in Cafe Purgatory
sipping $2 a cup herb tea from filtered water with no bugspray in it
or $4 a cup organically grown coffee
        from only companies that don't exploit Nicaraguans

How wonderful to have that choice!
Instead of hunting for a decent-paying job here
to pay the ever increasing rents
        to cover the ever increasing taxes
        here where the yuppies ever increase

You people walk around blinded by your focus
        on worlds so far removed
Deafened by constant anal-ization of the world inside yourself
Can't you open one eye and see what was in front of your nose
ISN'T

What's missing from this picture?
One less teenage hoodlum to have to pass on the street
nervously with your 'significant other'
If you noticed you'd think *changing demographics*

But what we're missing here
WAS
MY COUSIN

My cousin Ricky   was-blown-away
Right here on the corner where you live your 'pioneering' life

We buried him
while your face was buried in *USA Today*
B E Z droning in your earphones
        deafening your senses
            to such nuisance

& Ricky does not sleep nights no more
so he walks around in my dreams

He's not carrying the piece the cops found him with
He's just a boy with restless legs
Just a number now to read with your coffee & scorn
I mean scone

Sugar Blue, Harmonica Man

Sugar pours down
the hollow at the
base of my neck
over the scar
where a surgeon cut me
cross the ribs
in the center of
my sweetback
over my earring's
dance with the lobe.

Sonorous back roads sketched out
sighs of Southern sweat
stretched as long as each step
trying to catch up with his taste of
notes found in the savoring of
square holes.

His hands bounce in
shoo fly motion
while caressing
that silver box
as if it were my hips.

Two Dedications

I.
The Chicago Picasso

August 15, 1967

> *"Mayor Daley tugged a white ribbon, loosing the
> blue percale wrap. A hearty cheer went up as the
> covering slipped off the big steel sculpture that
> looks at once like a bird and a women."*
> — *Chicago Sun Times*

> *(Seiji Ozawa leads the Symphony.
> The Mayor smiles.
> And 50,000 See.)*

Does man love Art? Man visits Art, but squirms.
Art hurts. Art urges voyages —
and it is easier to stay at home,
the nice beer ready.
          In commonrooms
We belch, or sniff, or scratch.
Are raw.

But we must cook ourselves and style ourselves for Art, who
is a requiring courtesan.
We squirm.
We do not hug the Mona Lisa.
We
may touch or tolerate
an astounding fountain, or a horse-and-rider.
At most, another Lion.

Observe the tall cold of a Flower
which is as innocent and as guilty,
as meaningful and as meaningless as any
other flower in the western field.

II.
The Wall

August 27, 1967

For Edward Christmas

*"The side wall of a typical slum building on the
corner of 43rd and Langley became a mural
communicating black dignity...."*
—*Ebony*

A drumdrumdrum.
Humbly we come.
South of success and east of gloss and glass are
sandals;
flowercloth;
grave hoops of wood or gold, pendant
from black ears, brown ears, reddish-brown
and ivory ears;

black boy-men.
Black
boy-men on roofs fist out "Black Power!" Val,
a little black stampede
in African
images of brass and flowerswirl,
fists out "Black Power!" — tightens pretty eyes,
leans back on mothercountry and is tract,
is treatise through her perfect and tight teeth.

Women in wool hair chant their poetry.
Phil Cohran gives us messages and music
made of developed bone and polished and honed cult.
It is the Hour of tribe and of vibration,
the day-long Hour. It is the Hour
of ringing, rouse, of ferment-festival.

On Forty-third and Langley
black furnaces resent ancient
legislatures
of ploy and scruple and practical gelatin.

They keep the fever in,
fondle the fever.

All
worship the Wall.

I mount the rattling wood. Walter
says, "She is good." Says, "She
our Sister is." In front of me
hundreds of faces, red-brown, brown, black, ivory,
yield me hot trust, their yea and their Announcement
that they are ready to rile the high-flung ground.
Behind me, Paint.
Heroes.
No child has defiled
the Heroes of this Wall this serious Appointment
this still Wing
this Scald this Flute this heavy Light this Hinge.

An emphasis is paroled.
The old decapitations are revised,
the dispossessions beakless.

And we sing.

Carnality

Ah the lure of a bare shoulder
the charm of an undraped arm;
All flesh is carnal, pulses,
has warmth, vibrancy;
above all, has texture,
promises contact, animation,
perhaps pardon, tenderness.

Hell Night

For Patricia Smith

It's winter in New England:
ice patches roads risky in illicit thought,
old light falls off to strong nostalgia,
Boston freezes in Demeter's darker hour,
but not where we are.

It is Hell Night at the Ragin' Cajun Cafe,
where each dish
is spiced and peppered to screaming,
earth's burning fried and
sided with searing.
Hot ain't just flavor here,
It's God.

We roll our winter hands like tinder,
anticipating that culinary spark
that lights such exquisite misery:
when our eyes mist like spring windows,
our lips line with succulent scorching, and
our tongues long to loll elsewhere...
BRING ON THE PAIN!

As we wait for internal immolation,
it is announced that any patron
who successfully digests The Flamethrower,
a murderous Habanero casserole
guaranteed to conjure Castaneda visions,
gets a special medal.
Always sucker for wreath and wing,
a little tin victory on the Korean cheap,
We agree and order two portions.

Our first taste is as bland
as Sunday beige
and we curse the chef

and question his lineage.
But the heat tears along our tastebuds
to take its throne in our throats
and we stop in mid-conversation
to audition new vowel sounds,
oooooh awwww eeeeee,
from floor to walls to roof,
an agony as cinematic as
Backdraft, The Towering Inferno
and Drew Barrymore, truly believable
as an adolescent telekinetic pyromaniac.
By the final forkful,
we are crying like veterans
of a ten-hankie Meryl Streep weeper,
eyes screwed like new cats,
clutching our chests in a Fred Sanford exit.

We beg mercy of the other elements,
douse the hurt with wine and breathing,
and swear on the graves of relatives not yet dead
that we will never do this again.
Holding, cooing,
we wait the pain down to cooling embers.
I pocket my medal and
you order seconds.

I know you are not hungry.
You are far from hungry, now.
But are you beyond the rules
that protect the rest of us from the exceptional?

I think to switch to crossing guard,
arms splayed stop in mom's admonishment,
to show you lines you've blurred,
stories needlessly embroidered,
walk you some sensible shoe,
less is more.
Instead I offer the fat of my hands
in a worthless X benediction:
whatever, whatever, whatever.
And I see you rising,

beyond goal and challenge and
sad, West Side shadows,
over struggle and breaks and breaking,
to flame.
Flame circling you like a demanding pet,
draping your shoulders like a stole on a show girl,
flame curling thought, and
buckling gift, and
rendering all reward to memory.

I see you in flame.
And I wish you the balm of water.

For My Child Who Became A Man
In His Thirteenth Year

One night without ceremony
you became a man.
It happens all the time
in storybooks with
young warriors and knights
But not always in life.
Of you my son
I can testify.
You stood up,
wiry but determined.
You stood tall without notice
like something that had slept
a long time and suddenly had woken.
"I will love you no matter what," you pledged
as you set to slay the dragon.
It was not Chinese or Chaucerian,
not even Mexican.
But it was very real.
It did not die but was wounded
and retreated.

Later, it tried to return, apologize.
"Fine," you said, "apologize all you like,
but you cannot come back."
Together you and I moved
from the kingdom of scaly,
slimy things that I used to not
so quickly recognize and
that you at thirteen, with courage
and imagination banished
from our lives.

I Could Not Swallow The Lake

On the edge of the city
I sit and I am drowning
dizzily, gazing into the horizon's tropic

I dream that I am the Chinese brother
holding this lake in my mouth
During this, I see the twinkling lights cease to glitter
my moon does not reflect on the lonely sand

Bronzeville has a dull gleam
the white noise from the rushing cars on
the No-Longer-A-Lake Shore Drive
have stopped
and the skydwellers of the north
those who live high above the ground
are awake with insomnia and   gravity forcing them to the ground

There are no lake breezes to cool
my hot blooded brothers in Pilsen
Nothing to quiet the talk in Bridgeport
No waves to quiet the sound of intermittent gunfire
from the near west side

When I hold the lake in my mouth
I discover jewels hidden in the dry bed city
no longer exist
and this great feat brings
me no joy
Seeing the door to my dream
I awaken and exhale
relieved
I reel from the brightness of my moon
reflecting off this lake

Tired and disillusioned
I ponder city lights blown away

the candle of the Midwest
taking off with the Winds
and I fight the sadness that overwhelms me

I could not be born each day without it

I breathe only when the El train rattles my windows
when the reflected light from big city skyscrapers
shines on my face
when the bleeping of car horns call out to me like the baying of sheep

I could not be born each day without it

I could not swallow the lake

Millennium, Five Songs

I.
Black swollen fruit dangling on a limb
Red forgotten flesh sprayed across the prairie
Parched brown vines creeping over the wall
Yellow winged pollen, invisible enemies

Boluses without homesteads, grubs without a voice
Burrowed deeply into this land's dark, dark heart
Someday, our pods and pupae shall turn in the earth
And burgeon into our motherlode's bold beauty

II.
We're a seed on the manure, on the sole of your shoe
We're the louse trapped in your hank of golden hair
We're the sliver that haunts beneath your thumbnail
We're the church mouse you scorched with a match but lived

We're the package wrapped, return address unknown
We're the arm lowered again, again, a bloodied reverie
We've arrived shoeless, crutchless, tousle-haired, swollen-bellied
We shall inherit this earth's meek glory, as foretold

III. *(for Leah, my niece)*
They gave you a title, but you were too proud to wear it
They gave you the *paterland*, but you were too lazy to farm it

Your condo is leaking, but you're too angry to repair it
Your dress has moth-holes, but you're too sentimental to discard it

You're too bored to play the lute, it hangs on the wall like an ornament
The piano bites you, it's an eight-legged unfaithful dog

Love grows in the garden, but you're too impudent to tend it
A nice Hakka boy from Ogden, so hardworking, so kind

The prayermat is for prayer not for catamite nipple-piercing
The Goddess wags her finger at your beautiful wasteland

A dream deferred, well, is a dream deferred

IV. *(Janie's retort, on her fortieth birthday)*
The same stars come around and around and around
The same sun peeks her head at the horizon
The same housing tract, the same shopping center
The same blunt haircut: Chinese, Parisian, Babylonian
The same lipstick: red and it comes off on your coffeecup
The same stars come around and around and around
The same sun tarries in the late noon sky
The same word for mom: *Ah ma, madre, mere, majka*
The same birthbabe: bald, purplish, you slap to make cry
The same stench: mother's milk, shit and vomit
The same argument between a man and a woman
The same dog, hit by a car, the same escaped canary
The same turkey for Thanksgiving, Christmas and the New Year
The same three-tiered freeway: Istanbul, Tokyo, San Diego
The same hill, the same shanty-town, the same lean-to
The same skyscraper: Hong Kong, Singapore, Toledo
The same soup: chicken, though the veggies may vary
The same rice for supper: white, brown or wild
The same stars come around and around and around
The same sun dips her head into the ocean
The same tree in the same poem by the same poet
The same old husband: saggy breasts, baggy thighs
The same blackness whether we sleep or die

V.
Why are you proud, father, entombed with the other woman?
Why are you proud, mother, knitting my shroud in heaven?
Why are you proud, fish, you feed the greedy mourners?
Why are you proud, peonies, your heads are bowed and weighty?
Why are you proud, millennium, the dialect will die with you?
Why are you proud, psalm, hammering yourself into light?

Cloud

If you are a poet, you will see clearly that there is a cloud
floating in this sheet of paper.
  —Thich Nhat Hanh

Before you became a cloud, you were an ocean, roiled and
murmuring like a mouth. You were the shadows of a cloud cross-
ing over a field of tulips. You were the tears of a man who cried
into a plaid handkerchief. You were a sky without a hat. Your
heart puffed and flowered like sheets drying on a line.

And when you were a tree, you listened to trees and the tree
things trees told you. You were the wind in the wheels of a red
bicycle. You were the spidery *María* tattooed on the hairless arm
of a boy in downtown Houston. You were the rain rolling off the
waxy leaves of a magnolia tree. A lock of straw-colored hair
wedged between the mottled pages of a Victor Hugo novel. A
crescent of soap. A spider the color of a fingernail. The black nets
beneath the sea of olive trees. A skein of blue wool. A tea saucer
wrapped in newspaper. An empty cracker tin. A bowl of blueber-
ries in heavy cream. White wine in a green-stemmed glass.

And when you opened your wings to wind, across the punched-
tin sky above a prison courtyard, those condemned to death and
those condemned to life watched how smooth and sweet a white
cloud glides.

Twentieth Century Nod Out (2)

gargantuan effort bags hurt-stained eyes,
heat-cracked teeth and back spasms at the overstress
            of a vowel. chaos
has settled in and made itself to home
a concerto of coughs & moans fortissimo — rood music
            for the cash bereft
as titans clash in the space of a Hollywood toilet,
whamming psyches into last week.

it's another day of dancing at the holocaust
the same ol' cold blooded bloodlessness
enervating the unlucky the weak the poor — jes
another mundane bash to inspire upper-class yawns

the four horsemen have capped the fortune five-hundred
and the apocalypse is in the mail

Gabacha Encantada

The Amtrak winds its way through West Texas
Through what the Blue Eyes call "Wasteland;"
Puro mesquite, blue sage *y noplaltzines*
Con zopilotes circling the blue skies above.
Those blue ridges in the distance
Are unoccupied Mexico.
Over the PA system a Texas cracker voice
Is making like a *chingon chicharon*
As it proudly lists the Texas features
And historical spots.
West of the Pecos the millennia
Have cut through the solid rock
Cañones con sus escultras surealistas;
Estoy encantado.
Ay Viejita:
Porgue no eres conmigo?

El Comandante

Che, they're digging up your asthmatic bones like bloodhounds,
that same circle of guerilla hunters who lived far away
from cola-cola-less Vallegrande,
who now want sweet tourism dollars in the mountains,
where condors once passed above corn beer slopes,
sterilized valleys and
comatose mouths of 100 haciendas.

What will the villagers buy when golden visitors
leave behind glittering offerings and polaroids?
Will barefoot indian children praise
your former interrogator General Barrientos
as they push through a *supermercado* check out line
with bags of free trade interloper ho-hos and cheese whiz?

Their parents' faltering lungs ache,
with tracheas narrowed to drinking straws,
and nights remain cold as the Yuro ravine
where the dictator's army encountered
your ragged band of adventurers
that distant October hour of the ovens.

"Our sacrifice is for the future,"
you told seventeen *compañeros* tasting
the same defeat as the tin miners in Bolivia's dark bowels,
well before Spanish-speaking U.S. Rangers,
Ñancahuazú-trained informers, and an eye-in-the-sky satellite
transmitted your sainted rage against the machine.

After A Reading At A Black College

Maybe one day we will have
written about this color thing
until we've solved it. Tonight
when I read my poems about
looking white, the audience strains
forward with their whole colored
bodies — a part of each person praying
that my poems will make sense.
Poems do that sometimes — take
the craziness and salvage some
small clear part of the soul,
and that is why, though frightened,
I don't stop the spirit. After,
though some people come
to speak to me, some
seem to step away,
as if I've hurt them once
too often and they have
no forgiveness left. I feel myself
hurry from person to person, begging.
Hold steady, Harriet Tubman whispers,
Don't flop around.
Oh my people,
sometimes you look at me
with such unwillingness—
as I look at *you!*
I keep trying to prove
I am not what I think you think.

Mysteries

Uncle Bernard, U.S. Navy, Retired,
sits out in the yard on a make-shift bench
wondering why his toes still itch
on the leg that was once blown off at the knee
and tossed overboard with the galley waste
to feed the fish that prowl the deep
when he served at sea on a Victory ship.
And why it is, in his bed at night,
it seems that his wife is beside him there
with her long dark hair and her soft warm thighs
invading his dreams, interrupting his sleep
when everyone knows she's long since gone,
buried somewhere with perpetual care
and a marble stone, leaving him alone
sitting there in the yard on a bench in the sun.

And why does his son, who comes to visit,
have a leg like his leg that was blown off
and is now just a bone on the ocean floor?
And why does his daughter, who sits nearby
have long dark hair like his wife once had
and looks like her, and has in her eyes
the soft warm love that belonged to his wife?

And sitting there on this bench in the yard
Uncle Bernard, with the sea in his eyes,
wonders about his absent love
who, like the toes that are long since gone,
has never really been gone at all
but lies by his side at night until dawn.
And he thinks about immortality.

The Jungle

Packingtown was a heaven for hogs,
where pre-bacon pigs squealed up a chute
and Beef bosses collected tons of loot,
buried sharp ribs and big old hearts in sewers.
Sledge-hammered cows woke up from a stupor
just in time to be killed. Vegetarians
were aghast at the embalmed meat scandals
and practiced clean eating, much like Jurgis
trying to bust open the Beef Trust.
Sinclair aimed for the heart but hit the stomach
and that was his charm, that and his idyllic
breath, sweet as alfalfa sprouts and oat bran.
All of the universe died in the meat plant,
where packers prayed to a hollow hog-god.

A Cigarette's Iris In The Eye Of A Candle

For Sister Dianna Ortíz
Washington, D.C., April 1996

The White House gleams at nightfall,
a kingdom after death where pillars and fountains
wrap themselves in robes of illumination.
Light bathes in water; water basks in light.

There is a vigil across the street:
Sister Dianna in a sleeping bag,
back swarming with a hundred cigarette burns,
one ember screwed into her skin
for every upside down question mark
dangled by the inquisitors of Guatemala.
None of them saw the candle's iris
in the smoldering eye of a cigarette,
yet tonight candles encircle her,
flames like blurred hummingbirds
around her face, cheekbones
the cliffs of a hunger strike.
A cardboard sign at her feet says:
Who is Alejandro?

The torturers called him Alejandro, boss,
wiped their hands to greet him.
After the cigarettes, they burned her body
with phallic torches, invited him to join
the interrogation of the ripped orifice,
lubricated with blood.
Instead he listened to the cries
like a doctor measuring the breath. Later,
she heard him curse in midwestern wheatfield English;
without the blindfold, she saw an Americano, white as ash.
She leapt from his car on the way to the Embassy,
refusing the ash smeared across her skin.

Sister Ortíz simulated the kidnapping,
violated the Eighth Commandment
against false witness, said the U.S. Ambassador.
A sadomasochistic lesbian nun,
said a State Department official.
A case of delicate nerves,
said the Guatemalan Minister of Defense.
The First Lady sat on a couch with her
beneath a constellation of cameras,
careful as a hostess with a wine-befuddled guest.
At the press conference a chorus of spies and bureaucrats
crooned in soprano: There is no Alejandro, no Americano.
In Guatemala, the pit where they dangled her
still writhes with rats and dying fingers,
the cordillera of skulls swells and ripples across the map.

Now Sister Dianna keeps vigil on Pennsylvania Avenue,
sheltered from the drizzle of ambassadors
by a cardboard sign, the vowels in Alejandro,
becoming the eyes and mouths of the words
she once taught in the Mayan highlands.
Her silence is the bread she will not eat, her eyes
contemplating the cigarette's iris in the eye of a candle.
The White House is a burnished castle in the distance
where fountains thunder, but no one drinks,
where the word torture has been abolished.
From a high window someone peers,
a servant or the head of state, and curses in English.

Harry's House

I have no idea what Harry Grimes looked like
But I do know that he was an Englishman
He drank a bit, worked downtown, had a wife, a dog, no kids
And in the Spring
You can watch the woodland come alive just out my front window
Because in 1938, Harry Grimes built his house with no front lawn

Wild black cherry and ash trees, some hawthornes, and a pear
Stand where sprinklers ought to be

Each Spring when snow still lies in the shade
Tiny clusters of pure white bloodroot flowers no more than
    two inches tall
Poke through the cold wet black soil
When the sun shines, they spread their white petals to expose their
    butter colored genitals
They become a carpet of tiny white flashers teasing the cool Spring Sun
When the Sun sets, they close those petals and wrap their veined leaves
    around their tender privates
To become an army of little green bats sleeping rightside up

When the bloodroot petals drop, the may apples are ankle high
    everywhere
By the time they are knee high
It looks like someone planted a plot of funny dwarf umbrellas in my
    front yard
Each umbrella shelters one white blossom
And one green bitter fruit

Then the crocuses, the creeping buttercups, the hawthorne and the
    pear trees bloom
Just as they have bloomed in every woodland in Illinois since longer
    than there is memory
One tall linden arcs across my front door
It is bent in that arc by the Northwest wind

Harry Grimes planted a black barked maple just to the left as you
    look out the front window, see it?
A botanist told me that that maple does not fit this woodland scheme
Biologically, it's an invader
Maybe — but in the Fall,
That maple catches the morning light and it glows red-orange
It lays captured bits of fire down on the black soil for me to rake
    on Sundays
On cold Fall afternoons
I gather my final scraps of Summer

As I rake, my eyes water
From the smell of mold
And from the smell of dirt on the leaves
And under my breath
I tell that botanist
To go to Hell
For Harry Grimes

A Poem For My Wife While She Sleeps

While you sleep
rain plays our
window
like make-out music
for blind cats

Buses crawl by
purring and unloved
Televisions burn
snow lonely
in other windows
for other ghosts.
Night coffee
goes cold.
Penny candles
blink
from somewhere far
like China
like Cuba

In your sleep
foreign radios
shake slow
and oily
and even cooler
by the lake
and at the dark end
of the avenue
where the last
Kool is smoked under
heavy eyelids
and the gospel is
taught in
whispers and sign language
Even the tap dancer
tiptoes home
through sand.

Hummingbirds
hurl their silence
clear through the milky way
without
a single echo

While you sleep
yellow cabs
run
fast as leopards
Moon-chalk dances
on the el tracks
A moth lands
in blue hair
Pirates crawl into
dumpsters
and mumble
acts of contrition.

An old Greek
bakes pastries
and curses
the nothing
that becomes him.
An old woman
with bad eyes
strings her loom
her spoons hang
even as soldiers
quiet as ice.

In your sleep
the litanies
of the sidewalk
are written
in spray paint
and blood.
Circulation trucks
toss their bundles
of hard news
to empty corners

Sailors
throw up
at the train station
P-coats
turned up at the ears.
A dogfight ends
the winner
licks his cuts
A white rose opens
like a lover's mouth

While you sleep
moons abandon
stray places
and hide in
bird nests
and mail boxes

An old girl puts
on a housecoat
A young girl takes
off her dress
while guitar music
calls to crickets
Night rolls out
its dirty carpet
like Chinese silk
Night rolls its
filed dice
down rat holes
to the worthy
subways.

In your sleep
rain washes
the concertina wire
deathly clean
and the lake
laps quietly
at sandy feet
offering up

alewives
and smelt
too slow for the
breakwater
The ghosts of
grandmothers hem
aprons
and leave
a rosary
and holy water

In your sleep
I hold you
close as a prayer
and drift
to night
part of the
secret
deep and
blue.

No One Wears Hats Anymore

For Yvette, 1909-1991

The casket centered everything; three grey
women circled closer, friends who waltzed
through fifty years together, chatted brightly
at teas, charming in red taffeta, sleek in black
jersey, blue Dior satin off the shoulder.
They could not forgive her rude departure,

how she drifted into disarray, forgetting names
and thank you notes. Her lapse of etiquette
in dying first. They averted eyes from bones
draped in unflattering pastel, face framed
in too dyed black hair. Gloved to the wrist,
they are prefaced still by Mrs, neatly settled

under the wide brim of refinement. Yet some
great sorrow roared out that afternoon,
an unbecoming fury just as the light was gone.
You could see it in their eyes, the fists
their hands made. Of course there were no words
to say it, the cheat of being utterly awake and old

with no cotillions to dance in, and someone coughed,
and one was dizzy and reached out for an arm.
The whole thing was done on impulse, really,
all those years and no one wore hats anymore
and the husbands were dead and there was nothing
to be done about it but to walk forward to the cars.

From "A," the End of the Earth

Born in the refugees' tea cabinet of Darjeeling,
he's another Tibetan who's never seen Tibet,
sloping Himalayan foothills
form a tight corner where the world
whirls around the hungry child,
where he learns by rote
in missionary boarding schools,
other cultures, other languages,
reflecting faces that don't
mirror his own.

Chomolungma stands high over
a jigsaw puzzle of crowded kingdoms
trying to catch their breaths in the altitude,
and flex their borders at the same time.

The child grows up, leaves behind
the world's tallest mountain
for the snowy city with the world's tallest building,
to ring up tons of food for suburbanites;
perishables stories high go to waste,
after he'd been weighed to the ground
by meagre portions years before.

He closes his eyes
and can still see
Chomolungma from anywhere on earth,
lying a hair width below
where jets cruise,
as he can always see
the sun, *nyima,*
even in the night of self-exile,
the one not orchestrated by the Chinese.

But on this very end of the earth,
in America, the big "A,"

success stands more a rumor than a wish,
its myths spun like prayer wheels.

His fingers trace a half circle as he kneels
on the sandy shore of Lake Michigan,
where he's cut through every conceivable
number, encounter, alphabet,
and longs only for a new hemisphere to return to,
a vanishing point to the endless sky in *Kha Ba Can*.

Chomolungma — Mt. Everest in Tibetan
Kha Ba Can — Tibet in Tibetan

Magnolia

The old saucer magnolia, hollowed
by insects, was paraplegic after ice storms
brought down two of her four leader limbs
and nearly split her open. I hobbled on a broken foot,
my right wrist seized by arthritis.

                    But we both looked pretty

to the power lineman, stunned by the canopy
of pink flowers and a sunburst of gold flame
across my swimsuit.
                Scrub tree's interferring
with the power, ma'am,

                    he says and leaps
into the branches of the fast growing locust, chainsaw whining
through the foliage a V-shaped plunge
to the trunk, the *décolleté* sky
strung with a choker of lines.

                    Crowding that magnolia
and not in her class. Oughtta come down.

Within days, heat baked the moisture
from the exposed magnolia leaves and the tree
threw them on the ground. A carpet
of blossoms rotted under my feet.

In my hometown I tend my mother's grave, sweep
away with my hand the dead leaves and flowers
fallen from the huge southern magnolia
she loved, statuesque as a woman behind our name
chiseled in granite, who will stay
to lift the sky darkening over my mother's head:

                    umnachten,

I speak into the cool dusk, the German word better for going
crazy with darkness, for leaning into anything that protected her
from the light. There is space for me here.

> She would place me between the blush
> that still rose like sap in her cheek
> after long winters and the vernal change
> of light that turned me like a sunflower.

Perhaps it was the authority of his muscled hip
or the way he hopped to the branch above
on one foot. I should not have said yes

the way in some summers, wild for sun,
for the cleft of danger, I have
nodded willingness to such distractions and turned,
in disregard of something that needed
my attention, my help.
                                    I have lost a tree.
The brittle branches crack up the sky.
I have lost this woman.

Manifesto Discovered Under a Trillium

On the foundational dark silence
     of the forest
and without need
     of worshippers
our temples grow
         with architraves
of reaching branches that rest
across columns
     of air and live sap, decorated with living
friezes that show us scenes in the lives
     of leaves.

Therefore proclaim with the voice
     of moss
an inviolable protectorate
     of wrens
and another, other-continental,
     of toucans.

Confer most-favored status, for the trade in air,
on all remaining mountainsides.
         Array in fractal
regiments the plovers and winged fish-eaters
 to guard the weary shorelines.
         Administer
last twilights to rivers which, if they are still
believers, may be reborn.
         Patrol
the poisoned deltas and lakebottoms and seadepths
with bottom-vigilant finned inspectors.
         Sort
through the gull-shadowed garbage that has buried
jaguar nations
     of the badger, frog and trout,
and tie the old tin cans
     of rusting gold mines
to the tails
     of CEOs.

                    Lock down the wilding
IMF and transpatriotic corporations
on diets
          of clean water and animal crackers.

We hereby abolish the practice
          of board-feet and clear-cuts,
We herewith establish the free speech
          of bristlecone branches and song sparrows,
We hereafter will publish only anthologies
          of flowers,
We hereupon enjoin all ownership and use
          of man-made poisons.

Till the new republic
          of the rain in common
can celebrate the green tally
          of a one hundred per cent
turnout
          of the blades
          of the grass of the fields,
          of the leaves
          of the trees of the wood.

"the blooz man"

god is a blooz man

sittin cross legged
with an axe angled out his lap
lovin and revilin us all like a flatted third
pressed gainst the frets of pain

god is a blooz man

what got life and death
strung like strings
cross his lovers neck

hear him prowlin round the alley of our minds
tryin to find children cryin from fear of the night

now, god believin its his man given right
to ambush any bodies head whose coppin a dream bout him,
ambushed mine one time, takin the shape of a ghost note
while cooin fugues of rain from the mouth

a mouth
which transformed into
this dimly lit window placed eastward
in a backwater shack called sky

a window
i creeped to
peeped through
dug myself as Vishnu
sleepin on beds of lotus
dreamin of creation and crossroads etched in my hands

and at that cross in the road
before consciousness shattered that
vision to awakenings demand

at that cross in the road came the man i would be
my humanity began to expand
now i understand
that
i is the blooz man
the blooz man is i

i is the whine of all things terrible
and the scream of all things tremblin

i is the blooz man
the blooz man is i

i is the seraph whose wings beat hatred
and the demon who smiles redemption

i is the blooz man
the blooz man is i

i is the whisper which cushions
the broken body in the sepulcher
of tumultuous existence

i is the blooz man
the blooz man is i

i is the blushin flesh of the quiverin virgin

i is the ho who blows the dawn

i is the throbbin eye
of the battered wife

wonderin where
her husbands gone

i is the song of fatherless generations
who were sired by the loins of war

i is the comin of the bedouin
soldier bringin the smashin of heads and culture

i is the white sail blown

by the winds of profit
sailin on seas of black severed hands

i is the blooz man
the blooz man is i

i is the ornament forged
from all shackled human freedoms

an eagles feather trampled
beneath the hooves of final solution

i is the shamed thighs of all raped women
demandin the rapists death as retribution

i is the blooz man

a black
boot steppin
goose steppin
stompin down the doors of scapegoats

blooz man

the screamin
stream of ash
blackenin the skies of bergen-belsen
dachau and auschwitz

blooz man

i is the cuttin edge of the rusted blade

and the mouth of the gapin wound

i is the angry innocence of the questionin blood
demandin to be answered too soon

i is the baptism
inside the exorcism
and the mission eye

of my own myopia

the elegy of praise
that is buried within the fecundity
of all anathema

i is the fingers of dead lovers
who still tickle one another cross the mine fields
of war torn lands

i is the blooz man
the blooz man is i

bring me the tears
of a five year old son
wonderin if he'll
ever fill his daddys shoes at all

and i will give you
the soft eyed grin of a father
knowin that one day
those shoes will grow too small

bring me your
choir of homesong
sang in exile while your
feet trod the sod of the stranger

and i will show you
the star that will guide
you toward your miraculous
birth in the manger

i is the knockin
i is the door
i is that voice both
harsh and warm

i is the last bit of will
that pain cannot kill
a fine thread of sun

in lifes tapestry of storm

listen

to the jangle
and the discord
of my sonata

hear

within its pale
blue murmurrin
the thin cry of hope

listen

to the single
flower sighin as its fightin
through floors of concrete

and hear i split   wind
with this voice called survival

i is the blooz man
the blooz man is i

The Ladder

Climb me step by step if you don't want to jump.
(Subeme paso a pasito, no quieras pegar brinquitos.)
    —Renato Lombardi
      "The Ladder" ("La Escalera"), Installation,
      CreArte Gallery, Minneapolis

The blueberry pickers at the market
are angels in their stained clothes

offering fists. They've come from the sky
with those clouds, those berries

as if shrunken heads knotted with a kiss.
Somehow they're upon us.

Our different geographies connect.
Why would they come to a rubbled land?

Why would they descend from a place
where possibilities exit?

They step on the rungs for one foot,
then another.

Why would they want this *hard place to sleep,*
this *pillow for a stone?*

holding out their hands
to wrestle, to bless.

It Was A Turtle

It was a turtle moving slowly towards the eyes and hands
of an inaudible whisper — what we bring.

It was a turtle moving inside the arms as if skin
was transparent and could answer riddles,

devour secrets like tiny flies evaporating
in the snapping jaws of the turtle,

asking fumes from flowers to gather and dig nests for eggs touched
by wormlike fingers bottomed out with sleep and moisture,

the husband crawling toward wrinkled green layers
of the amphibian who let him out of its skin for years.

It was a turtle resembling the canoe moving up the arms,
crossing the vein in the elbow to shine on the lake.

How could it have been mistaken for a knot of thumbs?
Did it hiss when the proud foot pressed on its shell?

It was a turtle humming in the sand, vibrating
toward the simple cove where claws are cleaned to breathe.

When the firefly streaked into the trees, it was removed from
having to spark against the space where nothing emerges,

flashing over the head of the crawling monster resembling nightmares
where tainted bones frighten tiny men into becoming themselves.

When waste surrounded the deserted village, those men found
dozens of burned turtle shells in the cold campfires.

It was the one turtle that escaped inside the moss of a horn.
It was the slow progress of a vowel and a place to seem.

It was the turtle building upon its silence that pauses here.
When it moved, something floated in the air then disappeared.

Each recollection recounts the turtle coming back across the water.
Every coin of misunderstanding announces its tracks in the mud.

When the retracted head became an illusion, something replaced it.
When the shell was preserved as the bowl of ammunition,
    the world wept.

It was the turtle leaving its anger behind without knowing
    the story of scales.
It was the bright head emerging with the hiss that brings
    one stone syllable.

Fragments Of The Other

Chang See-Moy's mother, when pregnant with her, spotted a pangolin
on their small Malaysian farm and so built a fire near its hole to smoke
it out. But no other sign of the creature appeared until her birth.

*

stay home

*

The girl was born with the animal's features: scaly hairless skin, eyes
so angled she could not close them, in fact, she had no eyelids at all —
and had holes for ears. Anyone who saw the infant remarked how
like a pangolin she looked. That missing pangolin, surely. But the
father disallowed the mother to abandon her to the convent. *She is
our daughter,* he said. *No matter how ugly.*

she built a fire

She does not resemble any one
other than her sister
and even then no one else possesses
two extra toes, dark plates of skin,
an extra long clit —
a monstrous infant
blooms from a monstrous shell.

I am sorry I am so ugly. I am sorry, father.

The dominatrix fits the mask to the man's face
until *his* matches the shadows inside
the fascinated body. The real skin being
the skin that feels any thing sharp.
And where does *she* belong?

*

In Scotland, if the fruits hanging from trees similar to pear fall into water, they become geese; those that fall on grass remain fruit. Though on close examination one sees they are not fruit at all but barnacles. Barnacles filled with feathers.

*

stay home

*

Lick the instep of my arched foot,
suck the crook on my bent leg — you
will not do this for the wife.
And I will not marry to disappear.

*

stay home

*

The woman asked her son, *why*
do all of your girlfriends have black skin? Think
of the children.
She asked him to *stay home,*
help her hang the curtains —
to drop everything when the fire alarm
signals the village volunteers
so you and I can drive to the blaze.

ugly as a snake

The mother struck a match.

The mother wrapped a head-covering around See-Moy and hid her during the day. The girl listened to her little radio and from scraps of newspaper taught herself to speak and read Mandarin. At night she tilled the earth. But one day some people saw her without her covering and when they screamed she said to them, "I am sorry. I am so ugly. I am ugly as a snake."

Those fallen on the grass remain fruit.

Those adopted at birth still did not feel at *home*.

stay here

When Dr. Hsu called See-Moy to wish her happy birthday the *pangolin woman* sang him a song. *A clean sound*, exclaimed the Professor of Computer Science.

When See-Moy saw the sea for the first time she wrote her name in the sand with a long stick.

    *

She told the people, *I am sorry.*

He told his father, *I am sorry I love men. No really I am not sorry.*

her name in the sand

the tea scorched the roof of her mouth

exquisite as a snake

    *

Each time the mestiza took a lover, even after several husbands and even after her fortieth birthday — she apologized for what she could not be: *I am sorry I wasn't born in the North where it snows cold snow. Or, I am sorry my breasts are not small and firm like your sister's. Or, I am sorry I cannot remember which fork to use first.*

The mestiza's lovers did not understand her sorrow or her bliss — as if *they* could not speak *her language.*

There are no hymns. No hymnals.

*

The mestiza told him to mind his own business, go back where he came from, sink or swim.

*

there are tribes along the coast that —
*

When she stood at the open-mic no one listened so she softly admonished, *shut the fuck up,* and not a word was spoken until she completed her story about lizards on the screens of her grandmother's house.

The only rite of passage
celebrates the membrane. The roof.
*

The mestiza lies down on the Oriental and cries. It feels so absolute.

Pope Innocent of 1215 forbade the eating of birds during Lent. But Irish monks believed the barnacle geese were of *mixed origin* — part plant, part aquatic — and therefore could be consumed.

from monstrous shells

from a small farm in Malaysia

Home Depot

She is white vinyl go-go boots sculpting
Her cocoa legs into a brown river.
She is mini-skirted lust for sale.
Forty degrees warm, this peek at Spring
And if it were twenty, or minus twenty,
She would still be here strutting her body
As the man who tries to casually wear his shades
At one in the morning, keeps a long arm across the street
Watches as the Jeeps and Beamers slow down to take a different
Kind of look at the Home Depot.
She is walking up and down the treeless concrete
Making wholesome into whoresome
She is a wish for a home ... for her heart.
She walks the space near one part of the dirty river
Because even this water holds the promise of some kind of cleansing.
And even the many many showers she takes,
Even the higher taxes that come with gentrification —
Only a skipping stone away from her life and
The elevators that don't work in her building —
Only a cast-the-first-stone glance away —
From high paying jobs and expensive lofts —
All these
Only defer the hour of this night

She is not twilight
She is the deep time of night when cops look the other way —
Or maybe they just look, because it's free,
And power is a voyeur
On this orange-lighted stretch of no-place-to-hide.

The moon is sickled slit of light
Winking into the dark —
Eyeing her with stingy illumination, watching as
'home improvement' is given a
Wry-smile twist of meaning
And the cars swoop down like urban vultures.

She is the Karma you hope does not exist —
The prayer at bedtime you said as a child to keep you safe —

This is not the life she flipped through in young girl magazines.

And even if the cement grows up around her feet with every
    passing week
She will not wear your pity
Although you want to wrap her naked legs in it.

This is My Heart

This is my heart. It is a good heart.
Bones and a membrane of mist and fire
are the woven cover.
When we make love in the flower world
my heart is close enough to sing
to yours in a language that has no use
for clumsy human words.

My head is a good head, but it is a hard head
and it whirs inside with a swarm of worries.
What is the source of this singing, it asks
and if there is a source why can't I see it
right here, right now
as real as these hands hammering
the world together
with nails and sinew?

This is my soul. It is a good soul.
It tells me, "come here forgetful one."
And we sit together with a lilt of small winds
who rattle the scrub oak.
We cook a little something
to eat: a rabbit, some sofkey
then a sip of something sweet
for memory.

This is my song. It is a good song.
It walked forever the border of fire and water
climbed ribs of desire to my lips to sing to you.
Its new wings quiver with
vulnerability.

Come lie next to me, says my heart.
Put your head here.
It is a good thing, says my soul.

Nebula

The night before I left Tucson,
I sat out and listened to the trains
grumble past Sabino's porch.
It wasn't grating like you'd expect,
they hummed through the dark.
I sat out there until the sun came back up.

There weren't any trains from two until six,
but I kept hoping to hear something go by.
I counted five shooting stars and a couple
of roaches careened past the couch.
They were huge, almost the size of a frog.

Sabino's Rambler was parked in the dirt
next to his house, it was empty
of course, but I just sat there like that,
in the dark, watching for shooting stars.

Nautilus

You tuck your head under my chin, press your skull
against my jaw. At three, you curl your spine to fit.
I sit upright, arms filled with your angles. In the hours

before your birth, you rode the hard waves down, down
into the pelvis's snug curve, squirming in the press
of bone and muscle. I could touch the crown of your head

with a finger, but you came no further till the next
day. In the hospital crib, limbs sprawled, fingers
splayed, you staked every inch for yourself. Nadia,

you wedged the bone door open and I pushed you
into this wider chamber. When you run, your shadowed
scapulae flicker like buds of wings. But even now,

as in the first days, you seek hard comfort, an echo
of the bone embrace that held you all one night, till
I had strength enough to give you up to the world.

worship

the sweat and the throb
pentecostal feet and tears and love and
arms loose with the love and
the body is light and blur and touch and the tug
       of centrifugal force on the limbs
lifting, the body cannot stay
       in place against the earth
lifting parts of the body
one must concentrate on holding one's self down
as if gravity were a conscious act
performed to the ground and the voice
       the voice
is color and spirit and symbol of the senses
and mind and more joys not yet known
but to pass in communion
       raised in praise and tightened
breath heaved against the walls
the other fleshes and ringing celebration
ringing time and time and time and
skin and moment
and the luxury of an ephemeral time
not coming again, unique and self-aware
selflessly urgent, wet
uncomplicated by the future and outside knowledge
and some would say
       this is church

this is not church
       this is us in a club and
the touch is not a god
       but the touch is sacred and
the celebration is us
       outside a pagan rite and bedeviled
       not yet worried
still happy, giving theologians fits as byproduct
and carrying the charisma
       our electric each other
just beside our lips
like spilled red wine

2 Gals From Chicago

Brave & courageous
Never ending friendship
a true Chicago gal
big shoulders
big hair
big hearted

For 10 years now she do's me
the big spiral perm
several snippings
until it was short and straight
then blonde
then big & blonde
Dolly Parton blonde
& red
big red
red hot
then back to blonde
more blonde
and brown again

For 10 years now
I've sat in that
big chair of hers
memorabilia taped to
her mirror
3 kids   each
2 husbands   each
2 fathers   each

Alexis & me
2 gals from Chicago

forever

Alexis & me

Workfare

I.
Us orange
men and women out there
sweeping streets
wear mouths like words that
have been crossed out,
eyes forever staring south.

Workfare is nowhere, is
workfoul and silent howls
in a room alone
while they insist we must . . .
we were born to . . . destined to
work, no shirk, no quirks, Jerk McGurk.

Their bite is
Arbeit Mocks Freedom
is really what workfare's slavers mean.
Nofair. Mean. You got any idea
what it's like to clean gutters so
corporate heels don't slip on dogshit
when they cross from one boss
to another to make a deal?

II.
Workfare's workfoul, no soul, uncool, fool,
workfoul grows scowls.

Break the rules, take the tools, open hydrants,
get defiant!

Out of your jacket, don't just hack it, turn
your blood inside out

and wear the red proudly in the streets again.
Workfare needs

another rag than the orange of the slaver state
or the white of surrender.

III.
Enough victim — victory's what we want!
Enough martyrdom. The kings of corporate rackets
have put us all in straitjackets
but in our new bloodjackets of revolutionary sweep
see how the street's silent butlers are flaming open
to deconstruct rotten profits, buck by buck,
till workfare becomes workfair and everyone's
got a piece of the action called Tomorrow.

Remnants Performance (Life, Liberty, Pursuit of Poetry) Groningen (Cafe Verla) 10/19/98 3:21 am

Kiwi egg toilet paper nest floor after-gig Groningen
to be floor to have seen from below and supported
to have been through under all to have remained
poets their mouths milling grinding spewing sieving
time getting stuck between mind-sharp incisors' husks
light-biters, heavy-spitters, raked naked, oratorians
ejaculating pojizzarama bang garbage lids' wrenches
walls melt under-sound wheelbarrows scrape cerebrum
nailing meaning music arrow flight snip kite string
kiwi egg toilet paper nest floor after-gig Groningen
solid flicker gaping totality eke syllable crust gasp
one big dive off the white apartment building waterfall
a jet of language trail to Sirius Dogstar visiting recording
scientific data interbreeding with alien populace returning
everybody pregnant all in a single glance remember
to breathe it's a good thing spilling every idea into sheer
invention children pop out of your suitcase and sit there
obediently dancing and thrilled

Canticus Narcissus

Behind the body of a suicide blonde,
the theory of resurrection,
which is only, of course, a theory
but causes bodies to rise and float
like thin magician's assistants.

Behind each object, its universal shadow,
ancient shapes with no traditions
but a history of being.

Behind the storm, a freezing,
behind each death, two lives.
Behind the eye, an image as the mind
insists on having it seen,
mother for instance lying near death
with rouged cheeks the nurse applied.

Behind your desire, the starkness of the world.
Behind each ghost, eagerness and hunger.

Behind the news that can't be printed,
a cold rain falling, for this is not the world,
and this is not the dark. This is the word as mark,
where high in the attic of introspection
you can smell the *chimichanga*.

Before the thought, the sign; before the mouth, a name.
The world begins with the intimacy of distance
and ends with a crowding. It is then (then)
when (when) terrible and terrible
we are enamored of the sheer work of existence,
abstract meetings of flesh and flesh.

Instead of the age, a falling;
before the sheet, the winding.

Fat with winter, which here means rain,
we are on a future street. The sound of wheels
must mean: tusk of waking, birth of a pearl,
storm over park, rim shot timing.

On a hill overlooking a world,
these are the homes of the shining.

The Tongue Of Drunks

speaks of my sister
my father
my mother's father
and his also.

My grandmother bathes
a porcelain cup
shaped like a rose
filled with subtle
cruelties.

Each one speaks
of my grandfather
as he leans
on his only
arm
flicking a match
with two fingers
and a thumb.

One arm
speaks of chance,
left in wild grass
on a hill
in Richmond, Idaho.
The horse's hoof
lifts, frightened
by ten-year-old flesh.

Chicken speaks
of soup
in post-depression pots
with ladles,
A bird that always
simmers,
"You will never
be hungry again!"

My sister speaks
with the tongue of
drunks, as do
two girls
in the bathroom stall
beside me.
I cannot see them,
but the terrible roar
of their voices,
the loud sea of their
voices making
mouth and tongue
crash all at once onto
words

becomes the great cup
of words
boiling from my grandfather
and my father, my
sister, my mother's father,
his father, too;
My grandmother's
most exquisite hands
bend their petals
toward the man
who quietly beats her
with his missing arm.

The girl's
tremendous voice sobs
"Hurry! Hurry!
I'm going to piss!"
with the painful execution
of six cans of beer.
Her friend
behind the stall door
thunders back.
Their lives crash
like cars into one another.

Syllables kill themselves
on their lips.
They are my sister's.
I love my sister.
My father's,
my mother's father's,

And surely his father's, too.

Elvis In The Underworld

I'm the hillbilly cat from Tupelo
I was born in a shotgun shack
I walk a lonely street
and I have descended now
into the underworld

: : :

When I awakened from my death, I found myself
On the shore of a river, fast-flowing, deep, and cold.
The light was weak, it was an empty hour of the day.
From the other shore, a ferryman
Poled his way across in a ragged skiff.
I saw it was my Uncle Vester, my father's brother:
He who had taught me how to play guitar.
In winged boots and winged hunting cap
He came ever closer.
He boomed across the water:

Well, I'm the son of darkness
And the seventh son of night
My rhythm rises
From the swamp and hollow
My rhythm itches
Makes your feet, hips, fingers twitch
So that you've got to move.

Elvis it is time
To put away your spangled jumpsuit
And dust yourself with ashes
Elvis it is time
To lay down your guitar
And descend into the silence prepared for you
Elvis I have come
To ferry you across the tide of Acheron
To endless night, fierce fires, and shriveling cold.

And I replied:

I'm caught in a trap, I can't get out.
I will come with you, Uncle
But keep the boat steady as we cross,
So that the frothing dirty water will not stain
My blue suede shoes.

: : :

When you see them, tell them I am dead.
When you drink wine with them,
Tell them that I died while reading on the toilet.

It's true, what anxious mothers said.
I was the sullen voice of chaos.
I was the enemy
Of the Ed Sullivans of this world.

Uncle, where did it come from,
The tongue my hips spoke, my gleaming, sequined sneer?
My unborn twin, when he died in our mother's womb —
Was it his strength he gave me
Or the yoke of his futile rage —

I could feel the rage Ed Sullivan carried coiled within his neck,
The fear that bound his neck and shoulders.
They were afraid of me.
They cut my ducktailed hair,
They tried to make me their teddy bear,
Put a chain around my neck and led me everywhere,
Led me to Las Vegas, led me to the city of the lost angels,
Where I lost my soul, making such movies as "Clambake."

: : :

When I knew that I had come into the underworld,
I vowed that I would find my mother,
Who had been taken from me.

I hoped to sway Persephone
The way I tantalized the teenage girls of Memphis.
I hoped to lead my mother back up to the living.

But I can't find my mother
Anywhere down here. I walk a lonely street,
With this three-headed hound dog who follows me,
Crying all the time.

When you drink wine
With those who remember me,
Tell them that I cannot be their teddy bear,
Their hunk of burning love.
Tell them I am dead,
Tell them that I died while reading on the toilet.

： ： ：

Gladys, find your son
He's lonesome tonight

Gladys, find your son
Let him drink forgetfulness again

Gladys, forgive your son
Take him back inside yourself

： ： ：

I'm the hillbilly cat from Tupelo
I was born in a shotgun shack
I walk a lonely street
I have descended now
Into the underworld

I'm waiting for you here
In the place I've found to dwell

It's down at the end of Lonely Street
At Heartbreak Hotel —

I feel so lonely
I feel so lonely
I feel so lonely

Rainha Nzingha Reflects on the Absence of Justice

The President's elevator does not go
all the way to the top.
Do he ever think of Heaven?
I consider Heaven all my days.
His eye is on the sparrow
so much he misses me.

It's all on tv.
Hollywood!
How much do tears weigh
on a scale of diamonds? Dried like apples,
water stolen from them squeezed out.
Sadists I looked up
in the dictionary.
I've seen people who pulled
the wings off butterflies,
threw them up in the air,
commanded them to fly,
then trampled them beneath boots
til they glisten in the dust
like broken promises.

Bred man-sized cockroaches
in a filthy kitchen
like in that movie "Mimic."
They call them Mr. Man
who can be a woman
too. Cockroach.

I saw it on tv.
The Statue of Liberty my father, Mr. Williams,
said, "Give me your poor,"
"Give me your homeless." Like we don't have
enough of them already.
"Your tired, your huddled masses
yearning to breathe free." "Send them

all over here. And we'll feed these
Negroes gangred meat." My daddy,
Mr. Williams died laughing.

He occupied Europe after the War,
France and Germany.
Built back up what they tore down.
Like in that movie "Fraulein."
He was nice to her.

I want a Reconstruction, a Statue of Liberty
just for us
just us, that judges will look at without going blind
at the sight of beautiful darkness.

"There is no reality that you can understand,"
a guy told me once.
He was like that man on that episode
of "Thriller," the poet wrote about
who the ugly old lady pulled into the
mirror, where he stayed, with
her and a little girl.
More people got sucked into that mirror.
Screaming to get out
or come out
from behind a glass darkly.

I believe
you should be able to find
peace of mind at any church.
Not come away with a broken heart
that you didn't have when you went in
upon the age of reason.
Sadism is a religion, a game,
which includes many churches.
In some churches they hang a Man on a cross.
Then they look at Him,
and hurt other people.
Ain't no telling what they do to a woman
with a heart and a mind.

I wrote a letter to the Attorney General
of the United States
who never wrote me back.
I am not grandiose, but in a state
of urgency.
"Do I have rights?"
Silence.
How's that for a slap in the face?
Life, liberty, pursuit of happiness.

I want a Reconstruction, more than a Statue
of Liberty, a true nation under God,
just for us,
just us.

I want an eye for an eye, a tooth for a tooth,
a tear for a tear.

The murder of innocents calls for blood.

john lee: detroit special

there.
smash a metal string
under cotton hardened
fingertips seeking sun
of hammer, railroads, matchboxed blues
smoked between your teeth in song.

old man,
there was a time before my birth
when you scribed a motor crusted city into the air
scrapin up sound with more metal and sweat than
all the factories on jefferson.

in 67' you hoodoo broadcast
thirty year prophecy over a boogie beat:
detroit's burnin
and my father drove the east side
streets with a camera
to feed your proof of flames
into our family photo album.

now.
when your notes
take twisted chrome factory dreams
of cadillac deville and raise truth across our
eyes like a river of rust,

when you walk through suicide doors
clutching love of wild bent e strings
and smile with teeth white as
sunday morning cocaine,

these are the times we remember
how southern dusted shoes met asphalt and oil.
how we ransacked northern neon with
cardboard suitcase and railroad tracks.

how you can build a thing from the concrete up,
burn it like a match,
learn to live in the space
between your breaths.

The Poet's Mother

I met the poet's mother
in a coffee shop.
Frail, in her sixties,

she was sitting alone,
reading her son's book.
I asked if she was fond of poetry

(I'd seen the lines
broken on the page
as she rested the volume

to sip her tea)
and she showed me
the book's blue cover, his name.

I said, "You must be very proud."
She asked, "You *like* poetry?"
"Yes, very much."

she then put the book aside,
opened her leather bag,
and handed me two poems she had written —

one about a plane flying around the world,
the other about birds dying in cages.

Fin-de-Siècle Blues

I.
At seventeen I'm told to write a paper
on "My Philosophy:" unconscious Emersonian
clone, courtesy of my Father,
"There is no evil," that's what I say,
"merely the absence of good." I read the papers.
Where was my head? (In the clouds, like Father
and the senior William James.) I must have known
some of the bad news. No evil, eh?
Ho, Ho, Ho, Holocaust! Tell it to the Jews.

I wrote another paper, worrying
about the fate of historic monuments,
Art, not people, during World War II.
Give me that tired query from Ethics 101
concerning the old lady and a Rembrandt etching
in a sinking rowboat: which one would I save?
Now that I *am* one, still I have serious doubts
about saving the old lady.
Rembrandt would have won.
And if they could have been crammed into the rowboat
so would the French cathedrals and the Parthenon.
(There was some kind of screaming aesthete
Naked within my transparent ethical overcoat.)

But now, take Kosovo: Old ladies, churches,
children, art; all perish together
along with honor and philosophy;
the hypothetical rowboat long since sunk
in the polluted Mediterranean sea.
The century suffers entropy — and so do I.

II.
Well, it's been one hell of a century:
Endless lists of victims, Armenians, Jews,
Gypsies, Russians, Vietnamese,

the Bosnians, the Somalians,
torture and rape of the dissidents all over
the map; and as Time winds down
the music slows,
grows scratchier, plays off-key,
America chimes in with its own obbligatos:
what we did to the Nicaraguans, the Salvadorians,
diminuendos with Granadans, Panamanians —
and we're still hassling poor old Castro.

Whole continents go on living under tyrannies
till tyrannies give way
to chaos and criminality.
Is it the horror, or that we know
about the horror — this evening's blood
on the screen?
Yugoslavia, before our eyes, is Balkanized
to death; but today, brave us,
today we recognized Macedonia.
(Vasco is dead, thank God,
and how are you faring, dear Bogomil?)

Then we have AIDS...
Maurice, Tom, Tony, Gordon, Jim, Peter, Bill,
bitterly I mourn you
and wait for the next beloved name.
The red-neck senators who would starve the Arts
are a less efficient scourge.
We who are merely witnesses
to all this grief
also pay a price.
NOT AN ORIGINAL THOUGHT
(that's part of the price).
Horror numbs.
Violence, whether fictional or true,
is socially addictive.
NOT AN ORIGINAL THOUGHT
Serious satire undermined
by sexual and political
grotesquerie.
NOT AN ORIGINAL THOUGHT

So why go on? I'm blue. Boo-hoo.
Got those End-of-the-Century blues.

III.
Now to personalize and trivialize the topic,
As writers, what are we to do?
We gag on scandal, our lives are gossip fodder.
In our marginal way, we are becoming stars.
Never mind the work. Who cares for that?
Did the man who reinvented the sonnet
urinate in his bed one night when drunk?
Did our great fat nature poet
throw up in his hat?
Forget the revolution they created
with their raw confessional poetry;
it's the suicides of two women
which fascinate,
not their way of working
but their way of death.

O you serious men and women
who wrote your poems, met your classes,
counseled your students, kept your friends
and sent magic letters home,
your lives are pillaged and rearranged
by avid biographers who boast that they tell all,
so it seems you always reeled in a mad whirl
of alcohol, abandonment and sexual betrayal.
(I sorrow for the stain on your memory,
Anne, Randall, Ted, Elizabeth,
Delmore, John, and Cal.)

As writers, what are we to do?
Our roles as witnesses ignored,
our fine antennae blunted
by horror piled on horror,
our private matters open
to the scrutiny of voyeurs.
If we have wit and learning
it's met with the apathy
of the ever-more-ignorant young.

How do we hope to carry on
in the last gasp of the millennium?
Much as we always have, writing for one another,
for the friends we tried to impress in school
(like Tonio Krüger), for the dead father or mother,
for our first mentor, compassionate and cool,
for the dead authors who watch over us.
We'll write when bored in strange hotel rooms,
we'll write when the conscience pricks,
we'll write from passion, present or reviving,
making copy of our pains or perverse kicks.
We'll write if a cookie dipped in tea
transports us to the fields of memory.

But first of all we'll do it for ourselves,
selfish and narcissistic and obsessed as ever,
invading the privacy of those who care for us,
spilling sad secrets confided by a lover.
We take note of the café where Valéry took notes,
Van Gogh's yellow chair, the monastery
where Murasaki wrote, as Petrarch did,
in a room eight feet by three;
Name-and place-dropping, grooming our fur,
Fanning and shaking our peacock tails
(dry sticks rattling in the wind),
always, always ourselves our own mirrors.

The burden of our song: good luck to the young!
Let's drink (for we drink) to a better world
for them, if they should live so long.
As my father the optimist used to say,
"It's the unexpected that happens."
There is little point in being fatalistic;
Whatever occurs will be different from
what we anticipate,
which, to be frank, is universal doom.

Everyone who reads this is older than Mozart,
than Masaccio, than Keats, much older than Chatterton.
We're taller, handsomer, healthier than they.
So let's just count these years we've lived as velvet

as Carver said at the end — sweet Ray.
I'm blessed by parents, children, husband, friends
for now... Nothing can take that away.
NOT AN ORIGINAL THOUGHT
Call up Voltaire. Tend the garden.
Seize the day.

Meditations on an Olmec Head

Along stations of the sword,
Cross, & plumed serpent,
Some place between Xochipala
& here, a flotilla of boats

Nudges beyond monolithic green.
As if from among unlit mugshots
In a logbook of wanted posters
Chained to a post office wall,

This figure rises at daybreak
With *gumbo* & *yam* on the lips,
A stone that refuses to be
Dated. Big-shouldered

& awesome, the towering face
In a hemispherical helmet
Grows into a Detroit Lion,
A Chicago Bear on a billboard.

blood, water, pen, sword

...and she announces she will read her poem
out loud, right there among the dust
where the dog hairs have matted themselves
into a permanent part of the upholstery
though my eyes tell her I don't need her poem
at least not as much as I need another drink
to mollify me, she opens it up and it blooms
a story I've heard with my fist to my ear
no, not in so many non-conversational words
but about the bats she spends her days with
how they fly in circles and can't tell the difference
between artistic horizons and textbook windows
they suffer from amnesia by cracking the glass
in an attempt to touch what's behind it
she patiently flinches, slowly shakes her head
tinseled by her fourteen year old chains
her proud jewelry nonetheless binding...

> (the blanket stinks of a fat man's yeast
> laid out on the field pocked by horse hooves
> some other scent burning kindly with the breeze
> her soul never quite echoes between pear trees
> at any time only ninety-nine percent free
> when some ghost of a duty calls from the city)

...and this is why I am offended
by her blue lines, so perfectly parallel
how they sandwich her words like bologna
if she can't run naked through her dreams
then I at least advise her to write on it sideways
like a good dissident should

learning to swim

for a teacher in need of permanent vacation

his sleeves rolled up tight revealing veins popping
blood pressure rising like his voice
like the sound of a broken yardstick slammed against a desk
where questioning hormones reflect
the tension of yesterday's drive-by
glass shattered in rage from slamming the door
too hard to not notice
sweat veiling red eyes
tears escaping quietly to the floor
where one bright-eyed fourth grader gasps for air

she knows the right answer

she is drowning

The Other Hours

When I look at the ocean,
someone inside me sees
a house in various stages of ruin and beginning.

When I listen to the wind in the trees,
someone inside me, I don't know who, I don't know
if he has a mother or a father, a brother or a sister,
someone I don't know hears
the far voice of a woman reading out loud
from a book that opens everywhere onto day.
Her voice makes a place, and the birds
go there carrying nothing or the sky.

When I think about the hills where I was born,
someone — is he inside me? Is he below me? Beside me?
Is he the dismembered story
fed to the unvanquished roses?
Is he the rosebud packed in sleep
and fire, counted, tendered, herded
toward the meeting foretold?

Someone who won't answer remembers laughter
that sires the rocks and trees,
that fetches in its ancient skirts
the fateful fruits and seeds.

He won't answer, but I ask:
which of us is awake tonight?
If it's you, I must be the lamp
and its shadow. If it's me,
you're the native singing born inside me.

My Father Is An Excellent Dog

My father is fifty-five today
but he's riding mom's exercise bike
like it's a motorcycle.
He scrunches his face
and throats motorcycle sounds.
Changes gears
without moving.

With a quickness I don't remember
he leaps from the bike,
pivots and joins the couch.
He kneels,
peeking over its back
at his little audience.

He ducks slowly and disappears.
With a moment his head shows quickly,
and startles his audience
only because it comes with a new sound.
A barnyard sound.

My father is many barnyard animals.
Chickens and cows.
A rooster.
A duck.
A horse.
A dog. My father is an excellent dog.

My son opens his eyes wide
and takes two drunken backsteps
with each new animal my father becomes.
He waits for Papa Joe to smile
after moos and meows,
because Papa's smile takes the scare away
from the new sounds.

And as they play, and I play along

in my own space,
I catch myself laughing
and making my son's same faces
and remembering my father's face
his younger face
like mine today perhaps.

It was filled then, with more worry.
Filled then, with the hope and promise
on which he was always the verge,
and filled with the fear that it might not arrive
in time.

And now, thirty years later than what
he feared was too late,
the fear and worry were gone
and all the hopes and the promise
on which he was always the verge,
were here
fulfilled in one room.

And then with Papa Joe's smile
the littlest person I know
takes two steady steps
toward the biggest person I know,
And with Papa's smile comes my son's smile.
With brand new teeth and a giggle
that is small and sharp and new
and almost a laugh.

And I think,
"This is my father, this Papa Joe.
And I am his lucky son."

And I think, then — on this day,
with these chickens and cows and this
excellent dog —
on this farm,
with a choo-choo train running through
and a motorcycle in the back,
that I have heard these animals before.

When they were thirty years younger.
And beautiful.
But not like this.

Easter Sunday Morning, 1973: Maxwell Street, Chicago

For 'Little Pat' Rushing, Blues Master

"He plays to the Father through the features on men's faces."
   — Gerard Manley Hopkins

On Maxwell Street, in Chicago, Black,
And made with love, I saw You risen,
The Black Christ of Blues, and I knew
It was You for what happened in my withered heart.

I did not specially want the green to come,
But I was so taken in, I gave Your Son one
Of my last three dollars in the cigar box
He thrust at me, like an Usher at High Mass.

Basta! anyhow, Christ of my sorrows;
Why won't You just stay dead, please?
Why do You always turn up? In that Black
Electric guitar, or, in my absent, infant daughter's eyes?

Give me a break, Baby; take ten. Basta!
Basta! Basta! And You, John The
Twenty-Third, whose televised funeral also
Made me weep, like that Black, electric man.

Stop it! Stop it! Please, Black Pope,
With that electric Blues guitar, ripping
My heart out with every earth-born beat.
I've had enough. I'd like some sleep,

Some long, unfeeling sleep. Aren't You tired?
Your hair was conked, and sublime as John's mitre,
And the joy of having risen against all odds
Was in Your Black, and beautiful, and catholic face.

There was nothing like it anywhere in Chicago
This morning. You, and John, and the Christ
Who woos me from my absent, infant daughter's eyes,
All, merged into one, and the tomb of my heart

Broke open, and I rose with every ripping note,
Into Your Everlasting, into Your Blues-Blasting—LIFE!

Mistress Of Nothing

The breeze presses essence from the sea
presses malanga, hibiscus flower, white crysanthemums

The breeze sighs over Puente de Alvarado, over the river Grijalva
beyond Chontalpa, Las Choapas, and Teapa

Smooths the feathers of Lorenzo, the parrot,
who eats oranges
beside the road, on the outskirts of Oniaga—
as white butterflies shimmer in the air

The breeze carries murmur of harp
rumor of guitar

Beyond Agua Dulce,
beyond Juramento,
the breeze seeps into the House for the Child
inspires Salesia, enthralls dour Carmen,
calmly whispers
I am the Mistress of Nothing

On the way to Villahermosa, Tabasco

if you lose your optimism you're in serious trouble

For Leon Forrest, 1937-1997

i never knew the
coal that burned dark between us.
i understood your reinvented fire.
appreciated the dance, music and optimism in you.
recognized the writer, lover, professor running in you.
quietly this evening
i wished we had had winter-fights
lengthy talks, small arguments or deafening
disagreements stretching into the night of our imaginations.
i'll miss those nonconversations between novelist and poet.
i'll think of you while thanking you as i and others
continue our majestic journey
paging through the inspiring puzzles and prizes
of your language.

just aim and shoot
a love poem

bicycle princess
white beads in her hair
like her heroine
named after planetary splendor
is packin' heat
on the hottest day of our lives

"I'm gonna shoot you."

the sun kisses her silver 9mm
with the fashionable orange tip
courtesy of the barbie genocide collection:

a thirty-day bus pass
Ten W.I.C. coupons
three movie passes
a family album
with one photo missing

the empty space aptly titled
"your punk ass daddy_____"

an apology
for not being present
for first words,
to watch her tiny first steps,
or stop her from playing
"Drive-by Donna" on 51st Street.

thru thick plumes of
black & gray exhaust
she rides her bike
toward the liquor store
for a freeze pop
and penny candy

for a minute forgetting
she has to ask for help
to reach the top of the counter.

Loneliness

The kernels of my loneliness are too stubborn to grind
down to blue meal in my great-grandmother's *metate,*
too muddy for a dog to drink from,
too fast for a pill to net and tame.
I cannot climb the stairs of it,
nor offer it to my father's loom.
It is too ragged to weave a
rug to ease the night walks
across these cold bricks.

My loneliness lacks a plot.

It does not fit inside the stories my mother tells
about surviving an earthquake in Assisi, Italy.
It does not fit inside stories grandma told
about ignoring sirens, playing solitaire, praying
her rosary behind blackened windows in Cairo
when her pilgrimage to Jerusalem erupted in war.

Once I shouted my loneliness down. After my birth I cried out
to my father in Okinawa with help of ham radios and the
    Red Cross.

My lungs inflated like sails, distance was nothing.
I went everywhere, passed from lap to lap
of women who kept their loneliness secret
until it happened to me like the day of my first bleeding.

Capitalist Poem #55

What they mean when they say we're living in
the Information Age
is the Olympian vox populi of CNN

as global witness to our local forms of carnage;
the axe-clash of data giants in quest of net worth;
emerging markets maxing the sweet-pea amperage

that fuels the rise of the Cartoon Network
in a realm of flesh-and-bone cartoons
whose Babel of thought-balloons no longer works

and a new millennium dawns:
a thousand years of Scooby Doo,
a thousand years of oblivion.

For Your Mother, Whom
I've Never Met

Tell her
I would come to her door
Naked
As she would answer it
After an afternoon of housecleaning,
Naked at the sink
Cleaning yellowtail,
Steaming rice for dinner.

Tell her
I would let her, this once
Peel
My skin from me
Gingerly
Pull skin from flesh
Fold it over the foot of the bed
Like the overcoat of a proper guest.

Over noodles,
Fish flakes in tea broth
She could appraise
The composition of my bones
The resolution of my pulse
My veins, their history,
As distant as the blood of Moors
As present as the urban static
That keeps us from hearing
Our own hearts.

Tell her
I would come to her
By way of paths intertwining
A following of scents, intervening
Inside this widening map of souls;
I would come

By way of strength, not weakness
To meet the one that I glimpse
Naked
In my doorway at night.

Tell her
I would come
For you.

Twin Heartbeats

The twin voices of your heart are cotton candy
that melts in your mouth.
We wrap longing legs around words as if they were
crisp dreams that sizzle,
a survey of daydreams.
But they are only lukewarm coffee,
a cooling bouillabaisse.
You sip the taste of palpable air between us—
a temporary nectar—
& revise the tangible nights that pass for poetry
inside the quickening black suns of your eyes.
So many words rattle our days,
so many alternate voices in your head
& mine.
There are too many hands making demands in the morning.
The multiple voices of your heart, fragile as muted tongues,
become entwined garden weeds in the peripheries of
desert paradises and blossoming hells.
You wish yourself into multiple personalities, multiple selves.
You clone your thoughts as if baking so many cookies
on a well-greased wax sheet, baking your words, too,
into trifling desserts.
There are too many mad universes that you are over-busy creating,
overly sweet on the tongue, fallen soufflés that can't take the pressure
of your oversized hands.
You serve up cherry-topped sundaes, breakfast specials,
but we still sit like smart bookends at either end of the table
between the twin worlds you weave for you and yours & us.
I am caught in your facile computerese, the new language of poets
abandoning the typewriter for greener pastures, the fallow land
of no mistakes and no white-out.
There are too many contradictions in your eyes, a too-deep well
     of secrets.
The double image of your words shows such obvious signs of
     wear & tear
& yet I continue to fall under the spell of frenzied muscles & tongues,

an angling silence of twin myopia I acquiesce to.
As if there were more than the shallowness of empty air to complain to.
As if your twin hearts could break against the reassuring red glow
of the dawn and make that morning light
a sequence of real days complete with breakfast eggs and broken shells
that don't need daily mending, a virtual world that doesn't
    need programming
because you already live there
with too many hearts to count.

The Fractal Geometry Of Love

*Clouds are not spheres, mountains are not cones, coastlines are not circles
and bark is not smooth, nor does lightening travel in a straight line.*
— Benoit Mandelbrot

I. Self-Similarity

The smallest gesture
is the same as the largest:

when you placed your hand
on mine in that café, it was

the same as when you place
your hand on mine in bed

and when you look into my eyes
for a flashing instant, it is the same

as when you hold them until
we both burst into flame

II.   Broken but Infinite

Your eyes are not spheres.
My breasts are not cones.
Your nipples are not circles.
My face is not smooth.
Nothing between us
travels in a straight line.

If I were to attempt to
outline your sweet body,
I would be unable to do so:

if I touch it closely enough, so
closely that I trace each cell,

each cell's boundary, each
cell's connection to the next
cell, I would be measuring

your outline until the end
of time. And that is what
I am doing, lying here
next to you in the sun,

trying to move beyond time,
beginning my journey
to the infinite, my hand
slowly, slowly, slowly, tracing
the vast outline of your body.

III. Iteration

There is a kind of hunger
which satisfaction intensifies:

I touch you, I touch you again,
and again, and again, and again,

and with each touch I yearn
to touch you more, I am caught

in a feedback loop of desire,
touching and touching and touching.

Fasting

Seasons resonate through tissues and muscle,
and hunger changes sound and color.
Octave to octave like insects we dance
dizzied on spring nectar illuminance.
Summer's infectious mouth pours sour sweet blood.
Autumn drinks slow moonlight, lullabying
earth into the succulence of harvest sleep;
fruits and leaves begin to dream silently.
In morning, like prayer, we eat the faith of seeds,
and bury our heads memory deep.
In snow fields, in sleepless desperation,
licking the frost of your breath from my lips
is nothing more than instinct.
Loneliness is worse than eating bones.

The Peach Pit

fits in your palm like a round stone
picked up on a beach and slipped
into the pocket. The lines of
fortune etched on your skin fold
together when you close your
hand around it. They imprint
their mysteries on its humble
shape.
 Though pointed on one end,
it is too round to be called a tear-
drop shape, unless we mean
a tear that stays in the corner
of the eye and refuses to be
shed. The point is sharp, could
almost break the skin.
 The numerous
indentations are so deep they
give the illusion of boring down
all the way through to a dark
center.
 The brown-black of old
nails and wet tree bark, it is
a wooden heart at the core
of a ripe fruit. When you place it
on your tongue, the soft inside of
your mouth becomes the peach. At
first, its bitterness bites the tongue,
but gradually, a faint sweetness
rises to the back of the throat, then
spirals up into your head.
 On the globe
at the heart of a peach, the ocean
floor is full of trenches, deeper than
the Mariannas. The world is shifting.

Mater Dolorosa

I've never seen my mother's true face.
She is a constant blur made solid
by the mineralization of her worst fears
and petty jealousies.
Teeth bared, nostrils flared—
a Cubist visage
of distorted features
shifting through troubled dreams.
On rare occasions,
the heat of celebratory wine
would soften the steel edge of her eyes
revealing a bewildered peasant girl
aching to burn off the corrosion
that ate away at her life
and mine.
I often wondered what she thought of
as she struggled to keep up appearances
while we explored the mysteries
of the world beyond her.
Did she hear our laughter echo
in the hollow of her life?
Did she choke back bilious envy
as we played freely in our new home?
I could not bridge the distance
to her gated soul.
She held the key hidden deep within
the crust of salt that covered her wounds.
I'd come in from the dusk in dread
of the poisons that boiled down
during the heat of the day
waiting for the razored verbs
that would slice through my heart
as cleanly as the slices of meat
she placed on my dinner plate.
No guardian angel ever heard my prayers.

Halcyon Days

All summer long the sun
was our patron on the hill,
lavish and gaudy. The birds
rang their bells each morning
and we opened our door to bounty.
But now the sun has lost
its fortune and goes begging,
warming itself on our windows
in the lean late afternoons.

All of a sudden it is *our* season.
Green has moved to our side of the glass,
where the music is. In the kitchen
steam and fragrance rise from the stove.
We sit together and talk of the months
ahead as if they were books
we had waited to read for years,
as if the relentless farewell of our lives
had been arrested and we had another chance.

Red Dress

Midmorning, mid-February, mid-blizzard,
I pick up photos from a summer wedding
in Colorado and the first picture is me
all sass and flash in a red dress.

But it is the final photos on the roll
that I'd forgotten, taken several months later
of my lover reclined across my bed
in a blue shark skin suit next to my friend.

They are laughing as if they were in love,
yet if you look closely you'll see the boy is smiling
at the girl behind the lens although his hand
is on another girl's knee which seems appropriate to me

since in the end it was my skin he said
he felt nothing when he touched as if nothing were a feeling
and yet emptiness is never abstract when the body
drags, doubles its weight in the blue static of absence.

It seems some joke under the tyranny of gods
that these photos be juxtaposed. (The girl in the red dress,
the boy in the blue suit). They look nothing alike
and yet they fit together: she beaming; he beautiful
in his asymmetrical grace.

The girl looks so frivolous I want to slap her
though she'll never know soon enough a red dress
will never save her from sadness that soaks the bones
and burnishes the body to phosphorous.

Dazed by sun and alcohol, clutching a glass of cabernet
she looks like she could high kick her way to California
where at least absence owns the ocean and lovers
give back in pictures what they've taken in real life.

And who, when looking at these two, could ever guess
the red dress would become a wilted petal on the floor
in front of a locked door; and the boy's smile would slip
into history's index, his face turning away from the camera,

away from the girl behind the camera
as she continues to photograph
his back as he disappears into the blue
fugue of a day that never awakened.

Miss Saigon Protest Performance Queens

My friend Ken Choy
who loves Charlie's Angels
purely as any All-American
boyhood fantasy,
a queen from Orange County,
growing up with black bean bass
wafting to his room from mother's
kitchen; who in particular
loves Bosley — though this is
hard to believe — almost
without irony,
now pastes azure eyeshadow
delicately on my lids,
transforming me
to a Saigon whore.
Or, given my age and weight,
to a bordello mamasan
welcoming grunts, stoned
and sluiced and rich
with semen and Yankee
green. Oh
what girlish gifts could I
bring these nineteen year old
farmboys from What Cheer
or Macon county, stunned
by their luck at surviving
rice paddies near Da Nang
and the monstrous monsoons
that soak through bone and skull,
dripping the cerebellum ridges
where their All-American
nightmares reside. . . .

One Day In The North Shore

One day I was walking along some rail road tracks
Listening for bird songs, duck calls, grass rustling.
Trees hit themselves, and their leaves sounded an ocean.
I could hear dogs barking to each other some distance,
While my boots ground into small rocks and dry weeds.
It was a hot day, summer, a lost cloud here and there,
Lots of shadows, mine just ahead.
The tracks ended and I turned onto a road. I kept walking.
A car came by, fast, filled with kids my age, boys.
One of them threw an almost empty milk-shake container
At me. It exploded on my chest.
I remember that they laughed, called me "spic," their eyes
Looking at me through a back window.
I remember that I stood there, sweating, the smell of sugar
On me, sweet.

My Neighbor at 98

Reading newspapers, she checks the "Corrections" item first;
whose name they garbled yesterday,
who was wrongly identified as president of a bank.

Maybe someone was dead who is alive again
or the building they knocked down
will spring back up.

It's better than the rest of it: Taco Haven
murder, another scandal in the army.
There's a woman who's been missing 49 days.

Unlikely the Corrections column
will tell us: *Sorry, felt like seeing Eiffel Tower,
made fast getaway.* No, it's something gloomier than that.

Later my neighbor reads her postcards
dated 1902 (luckily her father saved everything)
from *Grossmutter* in Germany.

It takes awhile to translate each one
with a spyglass. A little late to know who went where,
the horse with the lame foot, how long it took to get over the flu,

but she likes it. Strokes of good cheer
elaborately frilled in a way nobody writes anymore,
but who can say? That luck has carried her till now.

Jellyfish

On vacation in sunny Florida, a little girl with a fluorescent
green pail reaches into the ocean and pulls out something
slippery and alive. "Daddy, look what I found," she squeals,
just moments before the jellyfish kisses the palm of her hand
and renders her unconscious.

Back home in Chicago, she spends her teenage years in a coma,
lying in a room with pale blue seashells stenciled on the walls.
In every room of the house, you can open a sliding glass door and
hear the ocean, but it is not the ocean really. It's just the waves
of Lake Michigan banging on the door.

Years later, her eyes click open like a plastic doll. She returns
to her life — unaware of the gap in time — until she notices people
walking down the street, talking into telephones that aren't even
plugged in. She notices how the earth has kept spinning and she
has only started her revolutions, and it frightens her. Her brother
tells her what she was missed while she was asleep, gives her
her 2,000 or so phone messages he has kept filed in a cardboard box
in the cellar. He tells her what he loves about modern life.

The girl, unconvinced, walks back to the beach she played on as a girl.
She lies down in still waters. She is delivered from evil. The blood-red
jellyfish do the rest. Amen.

You Are The One Who Names Us All

For Rozell Nesbitt

When the phone rang

I was out among old crusts of snow
cutting the first green miracle stems
of daffodils, the hooded blossoms
wound tight as silent bells, and
coming inside to take your call
I put those yard flowers into a clean glass jar
                           and brought it with us to the hospital.

A clean impersonal room where
you talked to us for hours
about road trips half a century old
and the boys when they were children.
You named the lost children some became
and their children, calling them to us there
where a hospital window framed
the tentative spring sky. We loved you
and when we said good-bye

                    we never meant good-bye.

You are the one we turn to
for stories: to tell us who we are and have been,
who we come from, and where to go next.
To scold, instruct, remind, comfort us, and make us laugh.
How can you leave? We still need scolding, still need comfort.

                    In church

the photo showed you leaning back, your grandson
in your lap, his eager hand making a grab
for the future. After service, loved ones flocked
together in noisy relief, the kitchen simmering
with casseroles and pots of greens, the house packed

with uncles, friends and kids, your students,
godchildren, yard cousins, all your boys and girls,
the ones you sheltered when others
turned them out, all of us
you built into women, built into men.

In that human heat the daffodils opened hungry mouths
like grief.

And already we've forgotten

what kind of car you drove to New York in '47,
what hat that uncle wore, and that second cousin,
how did she smile? We need to hear again
the journeys, the births, the couplings
and uncouplings. Who else will name
the grandparents and the great-grands and the babies
one by one, and who will tell us
why you went, who will describe that journey

who will tell the stories now.

We are planets flung out of orbit
the largest of us, and the small.
And so we hurt each other.
Forget to call.
Stars circle in unreachable sky
and people we love keep dying
while the rest of us stay busy.

There were ditches of lilies

and wild asparagus once

where now prefab houses line the asphalt streets
and you are silver
wind traveling deep green rows of cornfields
forgiving all the roads we call home.

Family Values

The man next door worked the line at Fords.
A tall man, he looked a bit sun dried
like a prune in spite of his bulk and pallor
and the red scar on his arm from the line.

Fridays after he got paid he went to one
of those bars that line up near the factories
to get a first shot at the check, where they will
cash them for no fee, and why not?

He never got home on payday until ten
or sometimes eleven or later. We always
knew because that soft voice of his
usually stuck in his throat like cotton batten

would rise, an electric saw caught in a board.
I would hear the curses hanging
like shooting stars in the bedroom's dark
and I would try to judge them for liveliness

originality and merit, for by the time
I was seven, I appreciated a good curse.
My mother was better, frankly, with Yiddish
as backup when English failed, but he was

persistent and wounded, leaking pity
like battery acid from every pore. If we
drifted to sleep, we would soon wake
because he would begin beating his kids,

the little ones first, and throwing them
out the grade door to crash against
the flimsy asbestos shingled wall of our
house. He worked his way through the boys

and the girl, with his wife slamming
out the door last. Then he would lock

the door and go to sleep, and we would
hear them sobbing, cursing, milling

in the driveway. No one ever spoke
of it. No one called the police and besides
didn't he have a right? He was the father
he brought home what was left of his paycheck.

They were like a dozen other families
on the street, no worse. The father who beat
his daughter naked with his belt; the mother
who withheld food to punish till her son

would go garbage picking for his hunger,
the cop whose wife lay in a darkened room
with bruises on her face. Families were strong
then, yes, strong as gulags

strong as the iron maiden embracing you
with her spikes, strong as cyanide
but killing you far more slowly. I can
hear still the bodies hitting the siding

under my window till the glass rattled
and their sobs on the close indifferent night.

Roses

Dissonance. Crepitation. My mind is clouded, scented with violets. My fingernails clean, shapely. The light hits the floor, just so, and someone bends over dead ashes black and silver in the grate. Today the I Ching says "Modesty," and "The creative force has a great refining influence."

Somehow I've plunged into wet denseness. Sound of dragon flies whirring past. Shadows of leaves on the sand. Faces of black maids dozing on benches in the sun. My father pats down my thin hair. I am his son. I fly away. Later my hands and feet grow so large they are embarrassing. Life is embarrassing, and so is his pale, flabby face.

I looked for so long for the tight buds/roses to pluck and plunder, unenfolding each petal, the scent rising to nostrils.

But she pulls away from me. Weak and stupid. Big eyes. Tender white thighs. Talks too much. Exiguous and sloppy. Finespun and odious. I can't get it out of my head—so much talk. All for nought.

The slimy cold mornings. Fishing in a boat, the sound of night birds still calling. In this cool hothouse birds still sing, but the phone is ringing, ringing. Got to go. Got to disconnect. I disconnect myself from stars and sky, plunge my hand deep into shit of earth, come up wanting. What's in there that we don't want to touch? Stanch it, stanch. Out of the deadened night flies the voice of nothing, so witty it pains one to listen.

Ain't it true, momma? Momma, make us a sign of the cross. Make us a cherry pie. Make it so I don't have to turn away and laugh so hard. You're on my side. I know you are. The abandoned hero.

Momma, please make us meek. Humble. It's what I always expected: the odiferous surfaces, the passages to hell. I am afraid. But it's alright now, more human. For better or worse. Prepare for your death. Or, like the old woman who saved boy scout knives, prepare to bribe a boy scout.

There is such a delicate balance between persuasion and force.

Me and you in the car. I heard you say, "take me, take me." Can I take you there. I heard you. I am Prince Fleur de Lys. All yellow buttons. I can take you, honey. Petal by petal. Your precious pink mouth. All of your soft, bruised surfaces. Your eyes stare at me, but you won't tell now, you won't tell. The future is in your hair.

Sharecropper

For John Henrik Clarke

I.
Tomorrows do
not rise
from memory; they
climb from dreams
pulsing in blood of today's heart
beats upon the anvil of
life.

II.
You are there, share
cropper of the struggle,
when all the long
distance runners
are gone. Your name
flags a tortoise
and crawls a thousand
miles after midnight.
You grew up with a
century and a nation;
you are muscle of America.
Your song flows through
its clogged veins of
avarice.

III.
I know you through your road
work: hitting the trail fore day
break, grinding out the extra miles
you find within a day.
I love
the way you shape your globe:
like a beating heart or a thousand
hands exploring the skin of tambourines.
The big question

makes you topple with song.
Epics of dish
washer women and penitentiary men.
Ascend
your vision and parade along Harlem nights

IV.
You are an age, an epoch
of flesh and blood no more.
Griot of down
and out dreams: peddling hope.
Griot of the road
maps of Wright and Malcolm X traveled.
Griot of opening
doors of dreams Nkrumah owned.
Possesser of the tongue
"Swing Low Sweet Chariot" owes its lineage.
You deliver the Black
mail, hostage to silence for centuries.
You deliver the Black
mail/special delivery through decades of storms
and downpours of blood.
You deliver the Black
mail through betrayals and lynchings.
You deliver the Black
mail through a century's life
span. You deliver the Black
mail.

V.
I take my name from foot
prints of the wind. A warrior
spirit travels. The world I know
is the world I make. The road
I travel is graveled
with hard epics. Foot
prints of singers. Who
run globes. Who run world
wide. Web sites of dreams.
I take my name from blood
steps you etched
on the odometer of freedom.

Fighting Fire

First the fire engines shake the night, the red blare
outside on their usual route past her building. Then

later, lying in sleep's nest, in the boughs of darkness,
safe on the creaking highest floor of the old tenement,
she wakes to a whisper in her ear. The night supplicant
as intimate, as desperate in request as a lover's *please.*

His staccato whisper raps on her neighbor's door. *It's me.*
From the hallway the whisper slides to her pillow. *Fuego.*
A trickle of sound like sand, a tired dry desire. *We lost
everything.* He talks to the ear of darkness, to the eye
of silence. *Tenemos nada. Nada.*

                                    She hears a hinge creak,
the jaws of measured speech. Then her room is emptied of
everything except what he has brought and left behind:
how the flames came close enough to lick her hand.

Next morning, under her window, the corner has a new rumor:
Fire set to smoke the tenants out, the wild bees honeycombed
in a house worth twice what it cost. Enough smoke, they drop,
stunned, and get swept away like dirt clods out the door.

    Summer mornings she looked out the back window
    from her grandma's house. The women stood shifting
    from foot to foot in the dirt, avoiding the eddies of smoke
    from their low fires.

                        The women, the ones they'd hired
    to do the wash, were boiling clothes in black iron pots.
    Hominy lye soap so strong and mean, it would skin your hands,
    her grandma said, so the sheets could be clean from every sin
    washed free, whiter than, whiter than, snow.

                                        The women
    stood by their kettles. They talked. They laughed. Every so often
    they poked a stick at what was seething there. It could have been

145

anything, brain, entrails, skin. It could have been the secret of life.

They hooked the clothes out with their sticks, and wrung them
dry as a chicken's neck. They wrung them until grief
fell in scalding drops back into the pot, and boiled again.

Early morning means Beatrice goes down and around the corner
to fetch drinking water. Half the women of the world are doing
the same but walking further, while she pays a dollar fifty a gallon.

A door opens at the corner's triangle. A woman is sweeping
crumbs of fire into the street. Inside there is clapping, there is
a song. At the threshold's altar Beatrice sees hands that flash fire.
Then the door slams shut.

                                  In grief she's rubbed her hands
together, hard, harder, like dry sticks of wood. Now anger
has smoldered a long time. What is she to do?

                                        Days she goes
to see movies at the mall, to sit alone with her neighbors,
watching disaster strike luxury shops in Beverly Hills,
a fire of molten lava pave the streets. Or skyscrapers
in New York explode into infernal bloom. Hell incinerates
the landlords who scoffed at warnings. The bad guys burn.

At night in bed she listens as sirens split the sleeping world
into homeless and the rest. She begins a mental list of what
she would try to save. She could pack a bag with photographs
and her poems, and keep it between her bed and the fire escape,
like a scuttle of hot coals to lug from place to place.

                                  Tinder
blazes up, light flickers over mouths shut on the word
nothing.

Crosses

For Li-Young Lee

I. *Power Lines*
The t-shaped utility poles
that outstretch arms to bear blackbirds
hang pregnant with power, *linea*

negra describing stomachs
about to contract, black bands tracing
bell-bellied flowers near bloom.

Like so many Frankenstein cartoons
not inclined to topple, and so
many St. Peters steady as

the hosts of black birds — like exposed
scarecrows, they stand impassive under
crow-yawp and pigeon-mourn, under

hawk-shrieked grievances and some
disemboweling lunar yowl —
Janus-facing moon, then sun again.

They tramp across prairie-grass like
stick-figure farmers with sticks on
their shoulders, balancing buckets

of fresh water, carrying more
than fire catching in dioramas
on ceilings, more than current

to urge unfeeling out of ice,
to sizzle cells, or run them, with
fricative sibilance —

but that's all we know of
electric charges, of crosses
delivering energy and light.

II. *Fourth of July*
Monumental crosses float out
of the cemetery, leading
an armada of sailboats with

gibbets and cruciforms raised,
but with sackcloth sagging. They mean
to tack but the wind lacks lungs

or luster and their streamers droop
like day-old confetti. They mean
to jib, but the gales flag as heat

curls cross-hairs into mirage.
This is where an ocean once thrashed,
its tides lifting sheets off

memories sleeping in sand. This
is where the jacana, our
Jesus bird, walked the water, her

feet impressing oversized stars
to drown the reflections of
setting husbands. And army ants

once locked limbs here, slicking a
seaway through. But when someone called
an end to quarries and quarrels,

he forgot to tell the fleet to
ditch cannons and row home — to get
back ahead of drying hostilities.

Now all these masts push upright
through the green, algaic seabed,
white like surrender.

III. *White Crosses*
Planting hard in the soldiers' graveyard,
brightly painted white crosses march
in formation into the horizon,

their flags drawing low to one side
like bandannas over right temples,
their shoulders hard at attention.

As they advance into the post-card
sky, a humming cleaves ground from ground
and Nile-blue blood churns underfoot,

liquefying bones criss-crossed like
so many birdfeet dried in tangled
mud, cross-striped like so many nails

and stars frozen at mid-blast. Grassroots
thrust up bayonets but these
grunts pad in peace, sighing slowly

through a Normandy shriek, silent
in a sunset burning like paper
on the skim of the River Kwai,

still as some miasmal orchestra
buzzes back from Gettysburg —
all tranquil here but for the river

of salt brought home by all their
dying trials, but for the red sea
joined by all these white crosses.

Confession

"Police respond to disturbance at circus."
    —Akron Beacon Journal 7/17/86

That night we told things we were ashamed of:
I crushed Grandma's antique Christmas egg; you
punched your sister — hard; and what was done to the cat
who will never be the same. We keep coming back to them,
going over the reasons everything happened.
It's like weighing a telescope, listening to a stone,
feeling for the breath of something whizzing past.

The Human Cannonball understands repetition.
Each night she flies half a football field to hit
the same patch of net and still
there's someone who tells her how to start the car.
            "Don't flood it, Arielle."
Each night she considers her options, then
climbs into the chamber. Later the two of them sit
in the kitchen before dawn. It's raining outside,
there's lightning without the noise. The man
tears the place up over something a long time ago.

At what point does absolution occur?
The priest slides the partition open and waits.
There is a moment
                    before a single word
is offered.

Each night, we retrace the steps taken without thinking:
the hole in the drywall, torn-up twenty dollar bills,
glass flung across the floor. This is what we sit with
in the kitchen after the cops leave.
Memory binds us. It holds us up like bones,
defines us like skin. How many have already
breathed the air in this room? It still sustains.
We say the words.

Weight

He was torn between
the lovable & the fuckable,

> tuning his heart & hard
> on the forked scales
> of male-lore, whammy-women
> & virgin daughters

Part passion, part passage
& part suspense...

> those "rise" years
> of lands & grooves,
> ...dick-tracings...
> unabashed bleatings,
> semen-rivers polishing mounds...
> & wounds...

In Patagonia

. . . neighbors include media mogul Ted Turner
and his film star wife Jane Fonda, who get away
from it all on an 11,000-acre ranch estate.
           —*Reuters, September 26 1997*

Captain Takemore needing no interpreter
slakes his thirst at the last pure waterfall
in Patagonia, smokes his cigar
in the last pure darkblue Argentine air
Mogul once now mogul-ranchero
Captain Takemore needs no interpreter
to command his situation to situate his satellites
excellently by design according to his will
under the Southern Cross

And here is Lady Takemore taken in her caftan
alongside the oldest hotsprings on the continent
foot tipped with silver toenails, dipping into jade
waters foamed with milk, yes
Lady Jane Takemore thrilling with the feel of it
taking all she can according to the plan

And here's the *triageur* of eyebrow hairs
and here's the secretary who registers the shares
and here's the personal trainer and here's the *chef*
                                    d'affaires
and here's her maid and here's his boy, because

You don't live in Patagonia all alone-O
you don't live in Patagonia on your own: no, no
When you get away to Patagonia under the Southern Cross
you can take Patagonia as a capital loss

Lady Jane: *I wish there'd be a revolution*
up in the U.S.A.
so we never could go back   we would just have to stay
down here in Patagonia

152

Down here in Patagonia
the real estate is wild
for those who can afford the purest air
the bluest for the fewest water
and the natives are undefiled.

Way down in Patagonia Captain Takemore
passes the cigars
Lady Jane leads the ladies to the mineral baths
the masseuse is extraordinary, Indian
you have to feel her hands
these people are so intuitive
Why can't there be a revolution
up in the U.S.A?

60/Blue Island

I used to have a job
　　where I would take the 60/Blue Island bus home at night
　　O say around 11 or 12
　　One night this goofy chick says all she wants to do is
tell every single one of us how much she loves us
　　and she also wanted
　　to ask for spare change
　　One night this skinny kid gets on he was 11 or 12
　　w/ an older woman his mother or what I don't know
　　right away there was a hassle at the front about paying their fares
　　the kid just walks up the aisle to where an older kid was sitting
and stops still staring at him
　　and the older kid is sitting there and staring back
　　and the little kid starts with some u aint shit whats your gang u aint
nothing type shit
　　his skinny arm flies out w/ a long skinny finger at the end of it
　　whats wrong w/ you man huh whats your gang huh
　　and the other kid suddenly cracks him in the jaw so that his bony
head goes snapping back on his chicken neck
　　but he really don't even seem to feel it
　　and he's saying now I'm gonna kill you you're dead whats your
gang
　　all this time the argument is still going on up front and suddenly
the bus is careening from side to side cause she has grabbed the
wheel and is wrestling the driver for it
　　everybody standing up out of their seats—let go of the wheel!
let the driver drive
　　until the driver finally gets the bus pulled over and is radioing
for the cops
　　while in back the two kids are still facing off the little one
letting the bigger one know he is fucking dead and the other
setting up for another jab
　　and I get up and grab the little kid from behind
　　for an instant feeling myself in that intimate space where the
lack of violence is like a vacuum waiting to be filled
　　He is as light as a baby in my arms and he struggles like a baby

trying to fight off sleep except he's telling me I'm dead too

I get him down in the aisle and sit on top of him

until I see a big cop coming through the door stepping up into the aisle his bulk seeming to take up the whole space

I get up and sit back in my seat. The kid climbs to his feet and throws out that long arm I am going to kill you motherfucker but in a calm even tone as if too exhausted for any emotion

The cop grabs him from behind almost enveloping him in his black jacketed size. No you're not he says quietly

and disappears w/ him off the bus

Later when the bus is moving again the other kid comes over to me and smiles and takes my hand in that kind of embrace where the wrist and forearm curve together We took care of him he says to me

My Nature Is Hunger

There were many Aztec goddesses associated with the earth and fertility.
The main deity was known as Toci, *but she was also called* Tonantzin, Teteo Innan,
Coatlicue, Cihuacoatl, Itzpapalotl, *and* Tlazolteotl. *She was the great conceiver,*
the principle behind regeneration, birth and rebirth. She was also represented as the
opposite concepts of decay and death, the taker of life — from the earth, to the earth.
In one of her many manifestations, the goddess was known as Tlaltecuhtli, *a frog-like*
earth monster with many eyes and many mouths at her joints. In this aspect, her
nature was hunger, a devouring deity, eater of hearts and of souls.

Anyway, don't come close.
I'm not harmless. I'm the ground swallowing.
I'm grass of thorns, insatiable dirt,
with green claws of vines and shrubbery.
My moss-furred tongue pulls you into entrails of roots and seeds.
I'm gaping petals like slimy smiles
taking you in, deeper and tighter,
filling me with a phallic spear of flesh.
My many mouths are many cervixes.
My corpse is a garden, covered in earth skin
with toes as mountains, a terrain of stone eyes
and watery grimaces. Enter here and die.
Leave and be born.
Every burrow, every crevice, every dank cave
is an eternal vagina that sucks, shapes, and also shuns.
Outside me bursts new life. Inside, a smothering death.
Out of my severed body the world has bloomed.
Man of woman. Woman of woman.
So come and get folded
by these coral fingers,
into my arms made of forests,
nuzzled by the music of my breath.
My eyes open toward the sky where man and woman
eclipse into God, and a priest, in someone else's skin,
opens you up to be taken by me —
fearful Mother, terrible Mother,
nurturer that caresses you,
and with a blink
shreds your flesh beneath moonless night.

Marvín Gardens

For Marvin Tate

He wears a boa to pull weeds. Neon feathers tease
lush leaves and even the shyest flower blushes
abnormally bright to grab his divided attention.

Black leather won't let him bend while he tends, so
he enters earth still standing, charming ground until
it opens soft under high-minded, high-heeled boots.

He could be a role model for the lay of bad lands, a
performance farmer ready to lend a hand with some
family planning for an exotic word dancer's dream.

Instead he'll groove on the truth of inner city plants,
dig his Ivy's urban girl dance, practicing the politics
sung in his rants and not keeping up with the Jones'.

Never keeping up with the Jones'. Telling the Jones'
to mind their own fucking business. It's his garden
and he'll wear whatever the hell he wants.

Bismillah Al-Rahman Al-Rahim
Pilgrimage
Dedicated to Michael Warr

The quintessential essence of evil entered in a "Nightmare Before Christmas,"
a black character that uttered words with a low, smooth voice and each time he spoke,
jazz played.

"Oh I come from a land/From a faraway place/Where the caravan camels roam/Where
they cut off your ear/If they don't like your face/It's barbaric but hey it's home."
            —Original lyrics of "Aladdin"

*   *   *

This blackness is divine
soft
comforting
and kind.
It encompasses
our anthill
that drives through the brown desert
barely visible in the gracious darkness of
a gentle-hearted night.
The moon radiates tenderly
marrying naturally to the potent ebony
providing a soft glow
for the exhausted Bedouin shepherd
who prepares his red fire
that smokes through gritty slopes to the awaiting sky.
The wooly gray sheep blend into the cascading sand hills
curving softly under the moon's glow
which surrenders to the dazzling coal night.
On the road to Baghdad
coasting smoothly on an impressible road
blackness
soothes us like the sweet smell of tea in Chicago's winter
and a mother's kiss consoling your fall.
Its guidance assures our way
as we embrace it flowing within us
leading us soundly
on our peaceful journey home.

Freedom Baptist

After Faith Ringgold's The Church Picnic, 1987

Seven families sit on home-sewn quilts
like cousins in Senegal whispering
among baobab branches. Woven baskets

take refuge under oak arms, as if the women
had just returned from market. But they
are dressed for Jesus in vivid patterns

of ruby, emerald and jade —
the ladies' hats stacked with fresh peonies,
the men in humbled suits and Sunday smiles

lean toward gourds of yams, collard greens,
biscuits. A breeze pins a leaf to Sister Maeola's
bosom and she starts stumbling a testimony,

I,I,I, that simmers like roots into a spiritual.
I love the Lord he heard my cry.
Hums spill over into waves, hallelujahs echo

tapping spines like God's blue breath.
Reverend Wright and Doris, the history
carrier, take to dancing: this is Freedom

Baptist's Picnic, Chicago, Illinois, 1909.
And an ocean away unripe fruits fall
from the baobab's grasp, as if they heard names.

In Praise of Some Women

I.
On the Death of Colleen Dewhurst, Actress
August 1991

Her voice —
like the thick buttered bread
Sister Alphonse made
when Dad worked at the convent,
and we lived in the apartment off the boiler room;

like country cream;

like the wind through the grass
on the west coast of Ireland;
like Lady Macbeth,
or Eugene O'Neill's New England;

like St. Therese of Lisieux
in an untouched photo,
her sleeves rolled up, at the laundry tub;
like Sister Elizabeth's Bavarian laughter
as she enjoyed her once a week beer.

Like Sarah Vaughan's singing;

her voice spoke the heart of humanity,
of Eleanor Roosevelt and Dorothy Day,
of women who love the poor.

II.
My friend Ruth Norrick died last year,
just as the thousands were leaving East Germany.
Ruth couldn't believe it;
she was an old line American Communist,
in the Eugene Debs and labor tradition.
Had she lived till this August,

she'd have had to believe it,
but would still have kept hope
for the people she pledged her allegiance to.

Mary Hutchinson, Catholic pro-lifer,
but all the way,
for the born babies too,
Pax Christi and everybody's rights,
called Ruth her spiritual director.

When Ruth saw the films an activist priest
had taken in Nicaragua,
and saw what some Catholics
were doing there,
she was amazed and delighted.

III.
Ellida Earnhart died this month too;
neither Communist nor Catholic,
but a people and nature revering humanist.
I wish I had known her better;
she could have told me how to deal
more efficiently
with those cans and papers
I can no longer just throw away.

Colleen, Ellida and Ruth,
you touched me,
you taught me,
the word, the world, and the people.

This Year's Flu

The pandemic of '18 killed a half million before it burned
out and they don't know why. No reason it won't come back,
sooner or later. Meantime? Sharon has an idea — interviews with
people who actually like their jobs, and not just for the money.
Title: *The Real Thing*. All effort must be directed. Twenty
below when the alarm goes off, and each year, more must be held
at a distance. The ten-year old and his friend, for instance,
who dropped a kid out the high rise window. Luckily, they were
sentenced for us; we must be safe. David's convinced that if we
didn't have children we'd live forever, and we did have our
chance, but we couldn't have laughed at the bar last night
without them. Or the old friend who's come to visit us after his
second divorce. Maybe that's the new disease. Tomorrow, we'll
meet for lunch, and this time I'll find out.

On Being Unable
To See The Sense Of Placing Something Beautiful
In The Lines Of This Poem

*Written after reading a survivor's account of how guards at the camp
paired up unusually tall prisoners with short ones so that the human waste they
carried from the latrines would slop out of the boxes and afford the guards their
morning amusement.*

If it is true that while imprisoned in the Little Camp of
Buchenwald, men and women were mismatched purposely to carry
entertainment back and forth in shit boxes held lopsidedly by Laurel
and Hardys made to move quick by the ordered insistence of familiar
guardians now become taskmasters in an evil play put on to pass dull
days by nurturing death to its final blossoms ... if this be the case,
there is no room in this poem for the subjective observations of a
hummingbird's wing or tulip sprouts.

If men have placed kerosene ointments on the skins of night
and torched black heaven's angels into howling hoots of horror while
Jesus on the lips of fair women hollered for their god-fearing men to
ignite cheery charring spectacles that needed to be illuminated for
example: "The black bugger didn't know his place." ... if this be the
case, there is no room in this poem for clever turns of a phrase or
language that makes language more important than life.

If removed from the proximity of consequences, celebrated and
comfortable internationalities, primping for the media on high-minded
pedestals, can still surreptitiously push technology to the ends of the
checkered earth, fossilizing the last outposts of indigenous freedom
while draping their global butchery behind fashionable pages of
promotional glitter ... if so,

There is no room in any poem for quip or pun or allusion. We
are past the days of innocence. No longer can we look on at the
elegance of art and chime romantic utterances to bird and sky.

Less than a mile from our Utopia sing the sickly tunes of
squalor and human shit hauled from pit to garden by mismatched

prisoners made to march in a miserable play put on by embittered guardians managing meticulously the modern manors of respectable corporate lords and celebrity kings who buy their beauty from poets who dare not tell them who they are.

No. This poem cannot contain, nor weave the glory of royal intellect into tapestries of needle-pointed grace. This poem's face is bony and burning. The smoke that circles from its nose stains the sky and even the birds have lost their will to sing.

No, this poem will not be lyrical. It is ugly and odorous, as odorous as that smell ... that sweet smell. Can you tell me? What is that smell ... that sweet smell we're smelling now?

The Deer

Mikaila clicks stubby fingers on the window
and the deer freezes, torn between its longing
for the ragged grass and the chill of sudden,
insistent sound. It stands in startled still-life
for a full minute while the three-year-old
behind the glass wails, *"Reindeer, come inside,*
I'm having oatmeal, I love you!" and whines
because her terrified new friend will only
stare in the general direction of all that fun.
We talk about whether it likes Barbie,
how we would teach it to sit on the couch,
dance ballet and eat popsicles. Meanwhile,
wind-blanched branches fascinate the deer,
it makes whole meals out of dryness and
light. It spends the entire morning chomping
the grass in full view of its new best friend,
whose mass of raven hair brands her a
tiny wildwoman, whose passions are simple
and untamed. They are warm to each other
past the window that separates them, though
each time the little fist bangs on the pane to
demand attention, the deer gulps and becomes
stone, its whole life moves to its heart. I sip
peppermint tea and watch this small Thursday
drama, realizing that I love a man whose heart
is torn that same way. You can't decide whether
to stay or leave, so you stay, stunned and alert,
but close enough for me to clutch at you in my
sleep, close enough for me to tap on the window
and beg you to come inside.

Elk Grove Village

Elk Grove Village,
Wisps of soft smoke.
A tall Elk rubbing his antlers
Against a giant oak.

In the village hall, the Councilmen
Make momentous decisions concerning
The future of this idyllic town,
While in the forest, a little to the east,
The Red Man

      makes his own plans

               concerning

    Con
       do
          min
             iums

              and

Three new nursing homes

    for sick   and aging

         Elks.

Blue Country

I am no longer lost in your blue country. From this wet hole I yell at you, I walk naked through your condominium, I am a magpie, a bastard, I collect pigeon eggs, I throw them at you, they turn into pigeons and steal your hair, I am happy that way.

When Americans die they will be forced to carry all of their possessions, box by box, up and down ladders, they will have to dismantle their priceless furniture and push the pieces through narrow doors, the angels will steal their clothes, no one will help them.

Because I am a train that will not run on time, I am a businessman with an empty briefcase, a salesclerk without a watch. I want to buy your house and fill it with mice, I want to turn your dogs against you, I am reading a spy novel, it is for your own good.

When you blow up the world, of this I am certain, you will have to clean it up, all the plastic and aluminum will poke at you, water and sponges will laugh at you, rags will laugh at you, you will cry out in the dark for wigs and shoes, you will look and never find them.

You will say "long ago" and "remember when."

And you will treasure my teeth like little jewels, and when I am laughing, you will see the sun for the very first time, you will stop in your red cars and wonder where did it go, all of these years, you will not know, because I will not tell you.

Herzog

He's a page in the family book, torn out by the frantic claws of
history. He's a dark spot, a footnote erased from the bibliography
of a 20th Century novel, written by businessmen and reputations, by
obedient wives and stentorian pastors, who preached God and civics
before a backdrop of Episcopal crucifixes and American flags. He is
missing, forgotten as quickly as possible by the complete chapters,
names like Johnson, Davis, Lockwood, and Stewart.

Herzog.

In the Mississippi Valley, in the hills of Central Texas, in the tidy
subdivisions of Los Angeles, Atlanta, and San Jose, in the middle
class neighborhoods on the north side of Chicago, in the postcard
towns along the Illinois River, where the family scattered over four
generations for boarding schools, colleges, first jobs and second
mortgages, he is forgotten, like a dirty secret, a spot on a bed sheet, a
drinking problem no one wants to talk about, a slight imperfection on
a dress shirt, where a tiny strand of polyester reveals the truth behind
a lie of clean white cotton.

Herzog.

In 1922, he scandalized an entire family of judges, mayors, and
real-estate men, who thought it could never happen to them, never
dirty the hands that dealt money and influence in the well ordered
meeting rooms of Mason Halls, Farmers Bank and Loans, courthouses,
and the meticulous living rooms on streets somehow always named
after trees — pine and sycamore, maple and elm. And they lived
comfortably there, in the shade of a nation where the rules were still
simple: invest well, give to charity, be civic minded, serve your
country, never marry a Jew.

Herzog.

From the postcard town on the Illinois River, they shipped them off to Chicago, where they were told to quietly disappear in a city where the streets seemed to buckle under the weight of overflowing Europe, all desperate in grinning grime and sweat. Herzog sold wine, shoes, insurance policies, and refrigerators to the Italians along Halsted Street, always with his eyes turned westward, towards that town on the Illinois River, where he would take her home, raise his children, and live in peace as an honest man should. In time, they both wore down with the impossibility of it. When they divorced in 1925, she was summoned home, where she would live until her death in 1963. He had given her two children. She would not give up his name. And it sifted like unexplained residue through generations until, in the end, there was no one left to ask questions. If there were, they would know this: that Herzog's heart was broken, but that Herzog did not die of a broken heart. That Herzog returned to Germany in 1927 to his family home in Hamburg and started over. That he died in Buchenwald in 1942. That his broken heart does not belong to them. They have no right to it. It is not their's.

Herzog. The Jew. The lover of my great-grandmother. The grandfather of my mother. Whose blood whispers in me when I least want to hear it, in muted syllables, crying to be heard over the other genes, muffled strands of DNA coming unraveled in the late 20th Century where the moral fortitude of America collapses under the weight of its own biology.

In October, I drive west on I-80 to where the Vermillion River meets the Illinois. I stand on a bluff and watch the last of the summer barges, pregnant and heavy with September wheat as they move like silent ghosts through the locks at Starved Rock, on their way to the safer waters of the southern Mississippi. Autumn paints the colors of violence across the riverbanks. Impish sycamores and White Oaks spatter reflections of shocking red and yellow over the water's surface. The river looks back as it always has, steady and assured, an elder moving through the centuries, collecting the knowledge that we are all impermanent, that there are some truths which we will never know. From here I can see the ceilings of river basin towns in a perfect geometry of church steeples and Greco-Roman columns anchoring tool factories and high schools, post offices and county jails. A red hawk circles above. As I turn to look up at him, he enters a noiseless dive and fetches a stunned cold water trout into his talons. It is over within seconds. A rush of liberty courses through my veins. I think of a great man who once said that history is on the side of us, that America carries the province of truth and righteousness on her side. And I believe this. That when my hands bleed, there is blood on my hands. But that history is true, that blood is the color of freedom. That people with my name have always been lucky that way.

God's peace be with you, Herzog. God's peace. Rest. My name is Christopher Stewart. I am your great-grandson. I remember you.

I remember you.

Mr. Orange

pulls down his pants in public places
like at the Laundromat and at open mic poetry readings
It is a never-ending piece in progress that he calls, "voyeurism"
I like Mr. Orange, he is honest, intelligent and clairvoyant
but he has a problem dealing with the present
Mr. Orange reeks of patchouli oil and sweat
he once told me how he saved a cat from being killed
by a bird, that he distracted the bird by feeding it catnip
while the cat flew safely into his arms
Mr. Orange and I have known each other for sometime now
while sitting in his one room flat above the old man's bar
he once tried to convince me into practicing chakra
and chanting the word, "oyah" repeatedly
this he said, would be good for my soul
from his new deck of tarot cards I pick the court jester
drunk on red wine while floating on top an empty champagne glass
that just like the insipid jester I too could live a carefree life
but first I must rid myself of negativity and unnecessary anger
music from the jukebox below starts to creep into the cracks
of the wooden floor; I can't remember the singer's name
perturbed by my lack of concentration
he's decided that I should leave while he returns to his makeshift
bed of nails, I must admit that sometimes I envy his esoteric behavior
it is puzzling yet intriguing to know someone who is so uninhibited
tomorrow we'll meet again for coffee and conversation
    at the corner bakery
and then we'll walk to the park and sit among the art-fucks
    and dope dealers
I'll surprise him with the name of the obscure soul singer
while he burns incense to keep away the many bad spirits.

I Have Seen

I have seen many a beautiful beach,
The whole world within tranquility's reach,
The mighty power of the human mind,
Which has within its grasp
The unity, the purity of total entwinement
In a world that can be totally changed
From the planet earth to the planet freedom.

I send my soul on wings of thoughts,
To reach and find and bring what I have sought,
To try to hurt no one, though hurt has been my middle name,
But never will I accept this part of the shame that society's
Hatred has brought upon all of us,
Like a thundering hateful, crashing rain.

I'd rather be like lightning, for it has no earthly gate,
It strikes the earth naturally, and not with deadly hate,
I'd rather be like thunder, for that is children's shouts,
I'd rather be a tear of sorrow than a smile of arrogance.

I know not which way my words will be borne by the wind,
But I do know that I plant the seed
Among all the people of my earth deep within,
That all can stand with a loving hand
And share our beautiful land.

I say I come to be with thee, my brother and sister,
I'll never hate the color or creed,
But rather fight the individuals whose lust for power
Has made them personifications of human greed.
Don't they know we only wish to live in total peace?

Gray Day In January In La Jolla: 1997

For Porter Sylvanus Troupe

the day absent of sun, troubles in over plush hill tops
threatening rain, cool hours mist towards noon
wearing gray shawls of vapor, patches of blue in places peek through
ragged holes punched in clouds, look like anxious eyes of scandinavians
worrying through their skins when they see snow storms coming,
in a place cold & white as anything imaginable, eye look

past green foliage here touched with hints of autumn shivering
like a homeless white man in a harlem doorway in february,
look pass white ice storms freezing the nation, all the way
    to the capital,
on martin luther king day, standing there on heated stone, bill
clinton takes his second oath of office, as rumors swirl around him
posing as vultures devouring an abandoned blood kill,

he lays out a vision for the future as good old boys dumped
like pilsbury dough into their rumpled suits fight back yawns, eyes
boring into the back of clinton's head like cold barrels of shotguns,
try beating back the cold of this day sweeping in from the arctic,
the cheers of the massive crowd are punctuated by gun salutes,
flags popping trembling wings crack over the capital,

as jessye norman takes us where we have to go, singing:
        america, america, God shed his grace on thee, & crown thy good
with brotherhood, from sea to shining sea
but we remember the reality of ennis cosby's senseless death,
    on this day
out here in the west, where everything seems so cozy and warm, where
time wears the laid back attitude of a surfer crouched on a board,

riding an incoming wave, eye see climbing up invisible ladder rungs,
deep in his imagination, the growing power of my son
porter's angular body, all arms & legs now, eyes peering out innocent
but knowing, laid back but cold, his mind calculating the distance
his thirteen-year-old body must conquer before he understands

the meaning of roads he has just walked over pigeon-toed,

clouds breaking across tops of hillsides, light shimmying in golden
blue, the sky widening into this moment bright as anywhere
clear & warm, the voice of jessye norman touching the blues, breaks
through the radio, her voice evoking history washes through
    this poem,
implants hints of lady day's warning of "strange fruit,"
as the threat of another storm gathers itself — as love

& hatred everywhere — north of here, above san francisco,
porter & eye watch shadows of clouds lengthening here,
see them spreading down hillsides like dark amoebas, mirth,
ragged as edges of daylight slipping toward darkness,
the air cool with mist now, the hour decked out in gray shawls,
cloud vapors now puffing up into shapes of dolphins, whales,

sharks cruising a sky cold as these waters off the coastline

Twist

For Zapp

Back when I used to be Indian
I am sixteen maybe seventeen
years old, drugged, driving the back
gravel roads with the white
boys, trunk filled
with beer. We close our hundredth
circle and park on a shining
tractor path at the edge
of a frosted field.
Thunder heavy from
the cassette deck.
Kevin bangs his head, babbling.
In the dew of his breath
on the window glass Steve traces
the names of all the girls he
wants to fuck. A door slams.
I wake up.
Upon his hands and knees Johnny
vomits algebra, football and
prom queens. I wrap him in my
jacket, carry him back to the car.
A deer staggers into our headlights,
an arrow through its neck. The blade
in my pocket dances against
my hip, digs in, begins to whisper
to my mixed
up blood.

Julia de Burgos

Poet and journalist, Julia de Burgos was a luminous writer of innovative, yet lyrical, poetry that documented her deep love for the people and culture of Puerto Rico. Personal conflicts, a case of untreated alcoholism and a deep sense of alienation contributed to her early decline and eventual death.

They found Julia cradled
in the concrete embrace
of a New York gutter.
It was a muggy day —
wind hot, streets empty,
sky overcast.

Her eyes mirrored
the gray above,
their warmth diminishing
the same way a bolero
ebbs to conclusion.
First a beat cop
tapped the business end
of a nightstick
against a shoe —
no response.

Then an ambulance
announced the world's end;
while paramedics went
about their business,
they had seen her kind
of death before.

On word of her passing,
the *Daily News* summarized:
unidentified Hispanic female
found dead on city street —
no foul play suspected.

Her bones clacked
their protest against
the waiting earth,
and the voice
that had stirred
a people
lost to silence
its power to rejoice.

On that fatal morning,
lady of sorrows
became an island,
a distant geography
far from Garment
District sweatshops,
Spanish Harlem flats,
beyond even the cadence
of her poetry.

Few remember that day,
when she plunged
headlong into darkness.
Only *Frida Kahlo*
could've painted *Julia,*
the way she died,
the way we don't want
to see her.

Half Moon Gate

Along the lake shore, a scream of gulls
          vanishes in the torn fog of a cool morning.
Jaws of the drawbridge, toothless, dank,
          swallow the sun. Afraid of your silence,
I edge close, ask why Elvis croons
          Don't be cruel to a heart that's true
on your tape player. At Half Moon Gate,
          past jars of fish eyes, ramen, kelp,
we search for an empty restaurant.
          I don't want no other lover —
I hear the curl of the lip, the forelock
          covering sultry eyes. Inside Three Happiness,
the waitress intones the lunch specials, a legato
          of vowels she steeps
in steaming oolong, black dragon's tea.
          Baby it's just you I'm thinking of.
I think of dark-eyed women whose jade pendants,
          brooches plumb freckled bosoms
as if good luck were red, green, gold stones
          rubbed once, twice, kissed.
In the back booth, brass laughter of X's —
          ex-wife, ex-girl, X marks the spot.
Would you walk through a rose bush,
          let blood thorns tear away
whatever ghost shadows you? Or me? Your *yes* —
          the triple-link bangle
you press in my palm. Mexican silver dreams
          of my thin wrist, trills the carillon
of your voice, your hand on my breast.
          Tonight my neighbor stews bell peppers
and onions, leeks and tomatoes in garlic sauce;
          roots herself to her notion of home
while her smoke drafts down my chimney
          over unburnt logs.
Behind my south window, the Seed Moon gilds
          my fortune free and clear.

Warriors

Warriors fall dead around us.
Murdered on corners buying burgers.
Outside White Castle they scramble for cover.
Five-O squats, poised for attack,
but can't find the source of the Gatts & crack.
Warriors fall. Their hearts stain the stairs
of their families' homes.
Cracks in the sidewalk channel their blood
to the next killing. The killings. The next
mother. The same mother. Her son dead.
Her sons dead. Cracks in the sidewalk
connect them. Systematically.
The killer is many killers.
In different colors & clashing cultures.
Chain murderers packed in Bigsby
and Kruthers. Bangers with nothing but bullets.
American fascists dressed in jurisprudence.
Cracks in the system hook them up.
A deadly circuitry hooks them to us.
Phone screams stab our ears in the night,
with chronic news of the warriors we love.
Poverty their serial killer. Delivering another
child unwanted. We watch them die young,
as they start to grow wise, threatening to be
more than a gangsta tribe. The loss lives
in Patricia's eyes. Tears of a second mother.
The stats of death not safe this time,
hidden in twisted headlines.
These are casualties we know.
Sticking like sights of Oklahoma.
Bombed and crying. Dust rising.
Children dying.
Their cities burned down everyday.
Ignited by things they do not own.
Detonated by things denied.
Kids becoming warriors.
Clashing in sidewalk cemeteries
for a pure breath of life.

To Malcolm X on His Second Coming

Malcolm X, alias El Hajj Malik El Shabazz,
alias Malcolm Little, alias Detroit Red —

> Deceased!

The coffin breaks, fingers wriggle through clay,
touch the light. A chiseled face comes full with flesh,
eyes roaming the landscape of his own prophecy.
Negroes in their Infinity's, Benz's, and BMW's,
chains of gold around their necks, fifty tons of gold
for teeth, sneakers handmade in the glass pavilions
of murderers. Hiphop stirring the empty souls.
Up from his tomb in our lost hopes, he stands
and prays into Allah's outstretched hands for mercy.

> This is why he came back:
> on a plantation porch, Lil Missy
> plays with Liza, offering her lemonade.
> "Liza, tell me again about them runaways
> you turned in, them bad bucks daddy
> hanged and cut up, lovely little Liza Mae,
> brown eyez, brown eyez."

At five o'clock in the morning in Baltimore,
in Philadelphia, in New York, in Newark, in Chicago,
the fresh morning water of showers falls, and
the followers of Elijah utter their morning prayers.
Allah the Beneficent, Allah the Merciful,
All praises to Allah, and the Nation of Islam,
Hope of the resurrection of the so-called negro,
comes to life, the life before the death of the Master.

> "Liza, where your mind, chile?
> me and the other boys had plans
> for bein free and coming back for y'all.
> My mama raised you from a little nothin,
> and you turned us in. Now we rottin

in some place with no name, cut up
like dog meat. Liza, where your mind?"

Malcolm walks in Harlem along the broken streets,
gathering mystified eyes. In Sylvia's he pokes his head in
and asks what food there is for the soul. Some woman
says "You look just like Malcolm X. You shoulda been
in that movie that boy Spike Lee made." And she goes on
cutting up custard pies and singing a gospel song she wrote.
Malcolm goes over to St. Nicholas Avenue, looks down
on the city. Afternoon shadows begin to fall like
the difficult questions of his father. Malcolm mourns
his mother, the abyss she fell into and could not escape,
the abyss of his genius. In a glimmer an angel settles
on his shoulder, as small as a pin but with a voice like
a choir singing. "No more grief, blessed son, no more grief."
Malcolm falls to the pavement, sobbing for Elijah.

Lil Missy sits in her bedroom chair,
sewing eyes on her doll, singing.
Liza listens to night sounds, afraid
of darkening the door to tomorrow.
Lil Missy says "Liza, come round here
and rub my feet befo you go to
my daddy's room."

In the Audubon ballroom the night he was killed,
Malcolm X saw his assassins rise amid a host of spirits
battling for his life. Demons and angels filled the space,
battling for his soft head, as his eyes took Allah's kiss.
His murder was a rupture in the world of the spirit,
the demons rushing desperately to name their position
in the African heart, where the angels fought to defend
God's voice uttering His own holy name, Allah.
Malcolm's head hit the stage like a giant stone
from Zimbabwe landing on Earth. His mind
took on its silence while his spirit was filled with song.
"Oh, blessed son, come unto me. Oh, blessed son."

In front of the Schomburg, Malcolm rises
above the city, his mind covering all of Harlem,
while he issues the manifesto:

On those who kill us/
Justice By any Means Necessary
On freedom/
Liberation is a Fire in the Soul
On the future/
We Cannot Capitulate to the Beast
On our Hearts/
Where Is Our Black Love?

Caravans form in the streets, unloading
the unconscious souls. The open eyes of the living dead
stare from windows and shops at this voice
that is in every doorway, this body that is the landscape,
as if the city is now flesh. In one moment he is there,
and then he is gone, letting their bodies go softly
back into time. Negroes wonder what has been
among them and is now gone. Malcolm sits on steps
on Convent Avenue, again just another man.
An old woman pulling a cart comes to him, touches
his head, and both of them vanish into Allah's wish.

The wise among us chant the filling of our life with life,
take this fragment of a gift from heaven and anoint
the heads of the young, who are our promise to live —

Teach Master, teach. Teach Master, teach.
Teach Master, teach. Wa Alaikum Salaam.

Any Day in June

the sweetest fruit is your smile in the haze of dawn.
the sweetest fruit surrounds us,
misted, electric,
sustains us through plodding schedules, timetables,
becomes the line of flesh we create again, at last.
lazy laughter tumbles from occupied hands, busy mouths,
song of late day's prayed-for caresses.
we roll and change positions, each now controlling
each consumed,
pulled by the heat of summer's music,
melody of skin colliding in rhythm,
we dance one inside the other
we walk the line of dusk, the soft crack between worlds,
almost dreaming, fluid,
lost in clenched muffled crying out —
sweetest fruit plucked from the tree of life.

clover tickles your thighs, your neck,
soft breathing returns.
I lay blades of grass in the shallow valley
between your breasts.
stars claim the sky,
the backbone of night, adrift.

A B O U T T H E P O E T S

Inka Alasadé, poet and lecturer, teaches a seminar entitled Poetics and Techniques of Writing Poetry through the Associated Colleges of the Midwest. She is a Medical Librarian in the Chicagoland area.

Elizabeth Alexander is the author of two collections of poems, *The Venus Hottentot* (1990, University Press of Virginia) and *Body of Life* (1996, Tia Chucha Press). She is presently a fellow at the Whitney Humanities Center at Yale University.

Michael Anania's many books include *The Red Menace* (fiction), *In Plain Sight* (essays), and *Selected Poems*. His most recent collection of poetry, *In Natural Light*, was published in 1999. Anania teaches at the University of Illinois at Chicago.

Eduardo Arocho has been published in *Open Fist: An Anthology of Young Illinois Poets* (Tia Chucha Press, 1993). He is currently completing his first manuscript, titled *The Colorful Children of Borikén*. Eduardo has taught writing workshops at high schools and colleges, and at the City of Chicago's Gallery 37 arts program.

Beatriz Badikian was born and reared in Buenos Aires, Argentina, and has lived in the Chicago area for the last thirty years, where she teaches writing and literature. Her work has been published in numerous journals, antholo-gies, and newspapers in the United States and abroad, including her full-length collection *Mapmaker*, now in its third edition.

Jim Banks has been a part of Chicago's performance poetry scene since 1988, and a poet since 1978. He is a former Green Mill Poetry Slam Champion and Chicago National Slam Team member, and has been featured and published in many venues and publications in and outside of Chicago.

Amiri Baraka is a poet, dramatist, political activist and has published 13 volumes of poetry, 2 books of fiction and 9 non-fiction works. Recent books from Razor are *Paul Robeson, The Black Arts Movement, When Miles Split,* and *Allah Means Everything,* and from Marsilio *Digging: The Soul of Afro American Classical Music.*

Mary Shen Barnidge was born at California's March Air Force Base in 1948, and is herself a veteran of the United States Army. A 1970 graduate of the University of Wisconsin (formerly Wisconsin State University), she is the author of two books of poetry and has been anthologized extensively.

Enid Baron's poetry and prose have appeared in numerous literary publications. She is the author of *Baking Days*, a book of poetry. A former editor of *Rhino*, board member of The Poetry Center of Chicago, and Ragdale Fellow, she trains teachers to teach poetry, and teaches poetry in the schools.

A lifelong Humbolt Park resident, Kim Berez works with area youth as an art therapist and Hip Hop Club sponsor. She's been featured at many local venues and edits *Starwallpaper*, an anthology of young poets.

Tara Betts writes and teaches in Chicago. Shortly after winning the 1999 Gwendolyn Brooks Open Mic Award, Tara represented Chicago as part of the Mad Bar team at the 1999 National Poetry Slam. She has self-published the chapbook, *Can I Hang?*

When Gwendolyn Brooks was awarded the Pulitzer Prize in 1950 for *Annie Allen*, she became the first black writer to win this prestigious honor. In 1969 she was named Poet Laureate of Illinois and continues to hold this post to date. She is the recipient of over 75 honorary doctorates, and serves as writer-in-residence at Chicago State University (CSU), where a chair has been named in her honor.

Dennis Brutus, a widely published poet, academic and activist, served time as a political prisoner in South Africa. He is Professor Emeritus of Africana Studies at the University of Pittsburgh. His books of poetry include *A Simple Lust, Stubborn Hope*, and *Still the Sirens*.

Lisa Buscani is a National Poetry Slam champion, and the author of *Jangle* (Tia Chucha Press) as well as two critically and popularly acclaimed solo shows, "Carnivale Animale," and "At That Time." She currently resides in Brooklyn, New York.

Ana Castillo is an award-winning poet, novelist, editor and translator. Among her numerous books are the novels *The Mixquiahuala Letters* and *So Far From God*. Her most recent novel is *Peel My Love Like An Onion* (Doubleday). She lives in her hometown Chicago with her son, Marcel Ramon.

Andrea Change has graduated from saloon poetry novice to veteran, and her words can be found in various publications including *Hammers* and *Stray Bullets: A Celebration of Chicago Saloon Poetry*. A recent graduate from Northwestern University, she has a son, Phillip.

Marilyn Chin's most recent collection of poems is *The Phoenix Gone, The Terrace Empty*, which won the PEN Josephine Miles award in 1994. She has received numerous awards for her poetry, including two NEAs, a Stegner Fellowship, and a Fulbright Senior Fellowship to Taiwan. She teaches in the MFA program at San Diego State University.

Sandra Cisneros is the author of *The House on Mango Street*, and *Woman Hollering Creek*, as well as two books of poetry, *My Wicked Wicked Ways* and *Loose Woman*. She lives in San Antonio, Texas.

"L.A.Blueswoman" Wanda Coleman's books for the 90's include *African Sleeping Sickness, American Sonnets, Hand Dance, Native In A Strange Land, Bathwater Wine*, and *Mambo Hips & Make Believe*, a novel.

Carlos Cortez began writing in the late 50's during the flowering of the Beat Generation. He has three books to his credit: *Crystal Gazing the Amber Fluid & Other Wobbly Poems* (1990); *Where are the Voices? & Other Wobbly Poems* (Charles H. Kerr Poets of Revolt, 1997); and *De Kansas A Califas & Back to Chicago* (March Abrazo Press, 1992). All are illustrated by the author.

Carlos Cumpián is the author of *Coyote Sun* (March Abrazo Press), *Latino Rainbow* (Grolier Publishing Company) and *Armadillo Charm* (Tia Chucha Press), and has also been published in numerous anthologies. Cumpián is an adjunct instructor at Columbia College Chicago in the English Department, and he also teaches in the Chicago Public Schools.

Toi Derricotte has published four collections of poetry and a memoir, *The Black Notebooks*, which was a *New York Times* Notable Book of the Year. *Tender*, her latest collection of poetry, was the co-winner of the Paterson Poetry Prize. She teaches creative writing at the University of Pittsburgh, and is a co-founder of Cave Canem, a workshop retreat for African-American poets.

John Dickson has published three books of poetry. He began his writing career as a short story writer, and when he began writing poems he had an early success with the Poesia Gradara, a poetry competition sponsored by the Italian Government. He received an NEA grant in 1990.

Denise Duhamel and Maureen Seaton have been poetry collaborators for about ten years. Their first joint book, *Exquisite Politics*, was published by Tia Chucha Press in 1997. Their collaborations have also appeared in *Boston Review, Prairie Schooner, Indiana Review*, and *American Voice*.

Martín Espada is the author of six poetry collections, including *Imagine the Angels of Bread* (Norton), which won an American Book Award and was a finalist for the National Book Critics Circle Award. Espada is a professor of English at the University of Massachusetts-Amherst.

Daniel Ferri is a former factory worker and studio potter who teaches 6th grade in Lombard, Ill. He is a successful slam poet whose teams have twice placed second at the National Poetry Slam tournament. He also writes commentary for Chicago Public Radio and for "All Things Considered" on National Public Radio.

Tony Fitzpatrick was born in 1958, and makes a living as an artist.

Suzanne Frank's background includes 10 years as a high school English teacher, countless years in the corporate world, and over 30 years as a private or public poet. She has read her poetry at many Chicago poetry venues, and is curator/performer in Women In Verse, a regular Guild event. She has been published in numerous magazines and anthologies, including *Stray Bullets: A Celebration of Chicago Saloon Poets* (Tia Chucha Press).

Cynthia Gallaher is the author of the book of poems, *Swimmer's Prayer* (Missing Spoke Press, 1999) as well as *Private, On Purpose* (mulberry press) and *Night Ribbons* (Polar Bear Press), which was honored by the Illinois Library Association and the Chicago Public Library. She was named one of the "100 Women Making a Difference" by *Today's Chicago Woman* magazine.

Lucia Cordell Getsi's four collections of poems and one of translations have garnered numerous grants and awards, among them two Fulbrights, an NEA and four IAC poetry fellowships, and the Capricorn, Stanford, and Neruda Prizes. She is University Distinguished Professor at ISU and edits *The Spoon River Review.*

Reginald Gibbons has published six volumes of poems, most recently *Sparrow: New and Selected Poems* (LSU, 1997) and *Homage to Longshot O'Leary* (Holy Cow! Press, 1999), a novel, *Sweetbitter* (Penguin, 1996), and other works. From 1981 till 1997 he was the editor of *TriQuarterly* magazine. He now teaches at Northwestern University.

Poet, percussionist, actor and activist Reggie Gibson has lectured and performed at schools, universities and venues around the world. Two of his works, as well as himself, appear in the film 'love jones,' and he was the winner of the individual competition in the '98 National Poetry Slam. His first full-length book of poems is *Storms Beneath the Skin* (nappyhead press).

Diane Glancy teaches at Macalester College in St. Paul, MN. Her newest books are *The Voice that Was in Travel* (University of Oklahoma Press); *(Ado)ration; Fuller Man* (Moyer Bell) and *The Closets of Heaven* (Chax Press) Tucson; and an anthology, *Visit Teepee Town: Native Writings after the Detours,* edited by Mark Nowak and Diane Glancy (Coffee House Press).

Ray Gonzalez is the author of five books of poetry, including *Cabato Sentora* (BOA Editions). The University of Arizona Press has reprinted his first book of essays, *Memory Fever*, and is publishing *Turtle Pictures*, a poetic/prose memoir, and *The Underground Heart*, new essays. He holds an Endowed Chair, The McKnight Land Grant Professorship, at the University of Minnesota.

Kimiko Hahn's recent books include *The Unbearable Heart* (Kaya, 1996), which received an American Book Award and *Mosquito and Ant* (W.W. Norton). A recipient of fellowships from the National Endowment for the Arts and the New York Foundation for the Arts, she received a Lila Wallace-Reader's Digest Writer's Award in 1998. Hahn is an Associate Professor in the English Department at Queens College/City University of New York.

Melanie Hamblin was born in Cairo, Egypt. Her writing has been described as imagistic and lyrical. She has read her poetry at a variety of venues in the Midwest and on the East Coast. Melanie is a member of the Tallgrass Writers Guild.

Joy Harjo, an enrolled member of the Muscogee Nation, has published many books including *She Had Some Horses*, *In Mad Love and War*, *The Woman Who Fell From the Sky*, and the anthology of native women's writing, *Reinventing the Enemy's Language* from W.W. Norton, co-edited with Gloria Bird. She plays saxophone and performs her poetry with her band Poetic Justice.

Jennifer Harris is a poet and fiction writer whose work has most recently appeared in *Fish Stories: Collective IV* and *The New York Quarterly*. She is the editor and founder of Jackleg Press (www.jacklegpress.com). In 1999, she was selected by the Poetry Center of Chicago to read in their "Emerging Poets" reading series.

Mary Hawley is a Chicago poet and writer. Her first book of poetry, *Double Tongues*, was published by Tia Chucha Press in 1993, and she was co-translator of the anthology *Astillas de Luz/Shards of Light* (Tia Chucha Press, 1998). She has performed her work at many of Chicago's poetry venues, and her work has been published in local and national journals including the *Notre Dame Review*, *Spoon River Review*, and the *Bloomington Review*.

Kurt Heintz is a native Illinoisan, a poet and media artist living in Chicago. He interacts with the poetic world beyond Chicago through overseas travel, the Internet, and videoconferencing joint poetry performances between Chicago and other cities far away. This cosmos converges at his participatory domain on the web, www.e-poets.net.

Batya G. Hernandez lives in Chicago with her husband and three children. She is currently writing a novel entitled *The Girl From Glencoe*.

San Francisco poet Jack Hirschman has published over 90 books of poetry and translations. These include *Endless Threshold* (Curbstone Press), *The Xibalba Arcane* (Azul Editions), and *Arcani* (Multimedia Edizioni, Italy). He is a member of the Labor Party and the League of Revolutionaries for a New America.

Bob Holman is the author of seven books of poetry, producer of "The World of Poetry," a partner at Washington Square Arts, and Visiting Professor of Writing at Bard College. He was co-director for the Nuyorican Poets Cafe from 1989-1996, where he popularized the poetry slam. He co-produced, with Josh Blum, the breakthrough PBS poetry video programs, "Words in Your Face" and "The United States of Poetry."

Paul Hoover is the author of seven poetry collections including *Totem and Shadow: New & Selected Poems* (Talisman House, 1999), *Viridian* (University of Georgia Press, 1997), and *The Novel: A Poem* (New Directions, 1991). Poet-in-Residence at Columbia College Chicago, he is editor of the anthology *Postmodern American Poetry* (W.W. Norton, 1994) and the literary magazine *New American Writing*.

A founding member of the Green Mill "Poetry Slam," Jean Howard has written, produced, and directed multimedia poetry productions. She is the author of *Dancing In Your Mother's Skin* (Tia Chucha Press), and has been organizing the Guild Complex's National Poetry Video Festival since 1992, with her own award-winning video poems airing on PBS, cable television, and at festivals around the nation.

Mark Ingebretsen edited and published *Hyphen*, a lit/art magazine, and hosted its monthly poetry and performance showcase. His work has been published in *Many Mountains Moving*, *Nebraska Review*, *Negative Capability*, and elsewhere. Born, bred, and educated in Chicago, Mark now lives in Virginia with his wife and daughter.

Angela Jackson, poet, fictionist, and playwright, was born in Greenville, Mississippi, and raised in Chicago. Of her poetry volumes, *Solo in the Box Car, Third Floor E*, won the American Book Award; *Dark Legs and Silk Kisses: The Beatitudes of the Sinners* won the Carl Sandburg Award and the *Chicago Sun Times* Friends of Literature Book of the Year Award; and *And All These Roads be Luminous: Poems Selected and New* was a National Book Award nominee.

Tyehimba Jess is author of the book of poems *when niggas love revolution like they love the Bulls*, self-published in 1993. He won Chicago's Sister Cities Poem for Accra Contest in 1994 and served as poetic emissary to Ghana in 1995. He was published in the anthology *Soulfires: Young Black Men on Love and Violence*, edited by Rohan B. Preston and Daniel Wideman (Penguin, 1995).

Richard Jones is the author of several books of poetry, including *Country of Air*, *At Last We Enter Paradise*, *A Perfect Time*, and *The Blessing: New and Selected Poems* (Copper Canyon Press, 2000). Jones is the founder and editor of the literary journal *Poetry East*, which is celebrating its twentieth anniversary. He directs the Creative Writing Program at DePaul University in Chicago.

Carolyn Kizer received the 1985 Pulitzer Prize for her collection *YIN: New Poems*. Her many awards and honors include the Theodore Roethke Award, and the Frost Medal from the Poetry Society of America for lifelong service to American letters. She has taught at universities nationwide.

Yusef Komunyakaa has published nine books of poems, including *Neon Vernacular: New and Selected Poems 1977-1989*, winner of the 1994 Pulitzer Prize for poetry and the Kingsley-Tufts Poetry Award. His most recent volume, *Thieves of Paradise*, was named a finalist for the National Book Critics Circle Award in 1999. Komunyakaa is Professor in the Council of Humanities and Creative Writing Program at Princeton University.

C.J. Laity is the Poetry Coordinator for the Annual Bucktown Arts Fest. His work has recently been published in the last issue of *Tomorrow Magazine*, in *Poetry For Peace*, and *Stray Bullets: A Celebration of Chicago Saloon Poetry* (Tia Chucha Press).

Poet/educator Quraysh Ali Lansana is the author of three poetry collections, a children's book and a children's musical, editor of two anthologies, and co-producer of a PBS award-winning poetry video. He is a board member and Artistic Director of Guild Complex.

Li-Young Lee was born in 1957 in Jakarta, Indonesia, of Chinese parents. In 1969 his father, after spending a year in jail as a political prisoner, fled Indonesia with his family and came to the United States. The recipient of many awards and honors, Lee's publications include the books of poetry, *Rose*, and *The City in Which I Love You*, as well as the memoir of his family's exile and emigration, *The Winged Seed*.

Billy Lombardo teaches and coaches at The Latin School of Chicago. His son, Kane, will graduate high school with the class of 2011.

Chet Long has published one volume of poetry, *This Running Sleep* (Windfall Press, 1968), and other poems in *The New York Times*, *Poet Lore*, *Prairie Schooner*, *The Commonweal*, and *Tri-Quarterly*.

Olivia Maciel is the author of the book of poems *Mas Salado que Dulce / Saltier than Sweet* editor of *Astillas de Luz / Shards of Light*, a poetry anthology from Tia Chucha Press, and a journalist on art and culture of Latin America. She is a recipient of the Jose Marti Literary Award.

Poet, publisher, editor and educator Haki R. Madhubuti (formerly Don L. Lee) has published 22 books. His fellowships and awards include the National Endowment for the Arts, the National Endowment for the Humanities, and the Illinois Arts Council. He is the founder and publisher of Third World Press, and founder and Director Emeritus of the Gwendolyn Brooks Center at Chicago State University, where he is a Professor of English.

Mario is one of Chicago's up-and-coming artists. His role in Chicago poetry has been well documented. Mario is Assistant Artistic Director of Guild Complex and is directly involved in the effort to free Mumia Abu Jamal.

Demetria Martínez is the author of the novel *Mother Tongue*, and a collection of poetry, *Breathing Between the Lines*. She lives in Tucson and is involved with the Arizona Border Rights Project which, among other things, documents border patrol abuse.

Campbell McGrath is the author of four books: *Capitalism*, *American Noise*, *Spring Comes to Chicago*, and *Road Atlas*. His many awards include fellowships from the Guggenheim Foundation and the MacArthur Foundation. Born in Chicago, he currently lives in Miami Beach and teaches creative writing at Florida International University.

Marci Merola is a native Chicagoan and has been writing short stories and poetry since she was very young. She is a freelance writer and volunteer for Guild Complex.

Author of *The Moon Cycle, Languid Love Lyrics, and Pastel Words*, poet Effie Mihopoulos has appeared in over 200 magazines and anthologies. She has published over 40 books under her Ommation Press imprint. She has been awarded numerous grants from the Department of Cultural Affairs, the Illinois Arts Council and the Illinois Humanities Council for her writing and poetry performances.

Patricia Monaghan is a member of the Resident Faculty of the School for New Learning at DePaul University, where she teaches science and literature. She is the author of two books of poetry, one of which (*Seasons of the Witch*) won the Friends of Literature award for poetry in 1993, and several books on mythology, including the definitive dictionary of the world's goddesses.

JM Morea's book *where the ending begins* was published in 1999 by nappyhead press. She is assistant editor of *dream in yourself* (Tia Chucha Press) and works as a resident artist in the Chicago Public Schools.

Kyoko Mori was born in Kobe, Japan. Her books are *Fallout* (Tia Chucha Press), *Polite Lies, The Dream of Water, One Bird,* and *Shizuko's Daughter* (Henry Holt). She is a Briggs-Copeland Lecturer in Creative Writing at Harvard.

Sulima Q. Moya was born in San Isabel, Puerto Rico in 1946, and her family migrated to Salt Lake City, Utah. She was educated at such schools as Crane Tech, Richards Vocational, Columbia College, and the Culinary School of Kendall College but never stuck around for a degree, preferring instead to go straight into community work as an artist and political activist.

Lisel Mueller is the author of six books of poetry, a volume of essays and three volumes of translations. Her book *Alive Together* was awarded the 1997 Pulitzer Prize. She emigrated to the United States from Nazi Germany at age 15 and has lived in the Chicago area most of her life.

Simone Muench is the associate editor for *ACM (Another Chicago Magazine)*. She won the 1998 Sheila-Na-Gig Chapbook Contest for her manuscript "Love's Apostrophes." She has poems published in *Crab Orchard Review, Southern Poetry Review, River Oak, etc.* and recently won an Illinois Arts Council Award.

David Mura's most recent book of poetry, *The Color of Desire,* won the Carl Sandburg Literary Award from the Friends of the Chicago Public Library. His first, *After We Lost Our Way,* won the 1989 National Poetry Series Contest. He is also the author of two memoirs, *Turning Japanese* and *Where the Body Meets Memory,* as well as a forthcoming book of poetry criticism, *The Limits of Our Vision,* from the University of Michigan Press.

Mexican American writer Raúl Niño is the author of *Breathing Light,* a collection of poems. He resides in Chicago.

Naomi Shihab Nye lives in San Antonio, Texas. Her books include *Fuel, Habibi, What Have You Lost?* (Greenwillow Books), and *The Space Between Our Footsteps: Poems & Paintings from the Middle East.*

Dwight Okita's latest project is a book-length manuscript titled *Serotonin City*, a memoir of three years of moodswings. His screenplay "My Last Week on Earth" was a finalist in the Sundance Screenwriters Lab Competition. And his poetry book *Crossing with the Light* was published by Tia Chucha Press.

Julie Parson-Nesbitt became Executive Director of the Guild Complex in October 1999. She is author of the poetry collection *Finders* (West End Press, 1996). She holds a Master of Fine Arts degree from the University of Pittsburgh, and her poetry has been widely published.

Marge Piercy is the author of fifteen collections of poetry including *What Are Big Girls Made Of?*, *The Art of Blessing the Day*, and a collection of her early and uncollected poetry, *Early Grrrl*. She has written fourteen novels, most recently *Storm Tide*, written in collaboration with her husband, Ira Wood, published by Fawcett in 1998, and *Three Women* (Morrow).

Deborah Pintonelli is the author of *Meat and Memory*, *Ego Monkey*, and *Some Heart*, and is working on a new novel, set in Mexico and the U.S. Winner of awards from PEN/Midwest, The Illinois Arts Council and others, she currently resides in Oak Park, IL, with her husband and daughter.

Sterling Plumpp is Professor of English and African American Studies at the University of Illinois at Chicago. His published volumes of poetry collections include *Blues: The Story Always Untold, Johannesburg and Other Poems, Ornate with Smoke*, and his latest, *Blues Narratives* (Tia Chucha Press). Professor Plumpp has received the Carl Sandburg Award and was recently awarded the Richard Wright Literary Excellence Award.

Minnie Bruce Pratt's *Crime Against Nature*, was chosen as the 1989 Lamont Poetry Selection by the Academy of American Poets, and received the American Library Association's Gay and Lesbian Book Award for Literature. Her other books include *We Say We Love Each Other, Rebellion: Essays 1980-1991*, and *S/HE*, stories about gender boundary crossing. Her most recent book, *Walking Back Up Depot Street*, is from The Pitt Poetry Series.

Rohan B Preston authored the poetry collection *Dreams in Soy Sauce* (Tia Chucha, 1992) and co-edited the anthology *Soulfires: YoungBlack Men on Love and Violence* (Viking Penguin, 1996). He received the inaugural Henry Blakely Award, given by Gwendolyn Brooks and 1998 and 1996 poetry fellowships from the Illinois Arts Council. A former arts critic for the *Chicago Tribune*, he is now theater critic at the *Star Tribune* in Minneapolis.

Mike Puican "grew up" in the performance poetry scene in Chicago. He's been published in *The Bloomsbury Review, Spoon River Review, Another Chicago Magazine (ACM)* and *Crab Orchard Review* and was a member of the 1996 Chicago Slam Team. During the day he works in marketing for a hair care manufacturer in Toronto.

Eugene B. Redmond was named Poet Laureate of East Saint Louis (IL) in 1976 and won an American Book Award for *The Eye in the Ceiling* in 1993. He teaches creative writing at SIU-Edwardsville and edits *Drumvoices Revue*.

Adrienne Rich's most recent books are *What Is Found There: Notebooks on Poetry and Politics* (1993); *Dark Fields of the Republic: Poems 1991-1995*; and *Midnight Salvage: Poems 1995-1998* (Norton). Her numerous awards for poetry include the Lenore Marshall/Nation Award, a MacArthur Fellowship, and the Dorothea Tanning Prize. Since 1984 she has lived in California.

Joe Roarty grew up in Pittsburgh, Pennsylvania and has been living in Chicago since 1974, and performing poetry since 1980. He has published a chapbook called *Horn*, which is part of a longer poem cycle called *Choruses*.

Luis J. Rodríguez is founder/director of Tia Chucha Press. He is also an award-winning poet whose latest collection is *Trochemoche* (1998 Curbstone Press, Connecticut).

Cin Salach has been a Loofah, Disgrace, Big Goddess, Diva, and one lip of Betty's Mouth. She has also been a slam champ, cultural ambassador to Prague, and featured poet in the PSA's Poetry in Motion program. Her first book, *Looking for a Soft Place to Land*, was published in 1996 by Tia Chucha Press, and she is currently collaborating with the poetically percussive musical collaboration Ten Tongues.

Melysha Sargis is a poet, writer, storyteller and educator. Her book, *Fountain of Youth*, is an Iranian folk tale for children (Rigby Educational Publishers). She received her BS in Psychology and Sociology from DePaul University and is currently attaining her MFA in Writing from the School of the Art Institute of Chicago.

Angela Shannon's poems have appeared in *Crab Orchard Review, Ploughshares, Triquarterly*, and *Water-Stone*, among other literary journals, and have been anthologized in *Beyond the Frontier* (edited by E. Ethelbert Miller) and *Catch the Fire* (edited by Derrick Gilbert). She is at work on an inaugural collection of poetry entitled *Rootwoman*.

John Sheehan, retired high school and college teacher, was a member of the Chicago Poetry Ensemble, and has read and recited his poetry many times, with the Ensemble or alone, at venues throughout Chicago and northwest Indiana. He is the author of two books of poetry, *Elsewhere Indiana* and *Leaving Gary*. A resident of Gary from 1968 until 1996, he now lives in Portage, Indiana.

Barry Silesky is author of *One Thing That Can Save Us* (Coffee House Press), *The New Tenants* (eye of the comet press), a biography of Lawrence Ferlinghetti (Warner Books), and poems and prose in many magazines. He is editor of *ACM*, and currently at work on the biography of John Gardner (for Algonquin Books).

Marc (So What!) Smith originated the Uptown Poetry Slam and is known as the Slampapi of the international slam poetry movement. He is the author of *Crowdpleaser* from Collage Press in Chicago.

Patricia Smith, an award-winning journalist and poet, is the author of three books of poetry — *Close to Death; Big Towns, Big Talk;* and *Life According to Motown* — and has performed at festivals from Brazil to Ireland. A four-time National Poetry Slam champion, she also co-authored *Africans in America*, the companion book to PBS' groundbreaking series.

John Starrs was first published in John Logan's now famous magazine, *Choice*. Pam Barrie later put out a book of his poems as an art book called *The Suburban Poems*. With partner David Hernandez, John has done a lot of performance poetry gigs. He is presently hosting a poetry venue called the Higher Ground Poets at Coffee Chicago.

Hugh Steinberg's poetry has appeared in *Grand Street, Poetry, APR* and *Epoch*. He received an MFA from the University of Arizona in 1993, and from 1995-97 lived in Chicago, where he was a member of Tia Chucha's editorial board. A recipient of a Wallace Stegner fellowship, he is a board member of Small Press Traffic. He lives in San Francisco, where he teaches at California College of Arts and Crafts.

Christopher Stewart has read his work in poetry venues, libraries, museums, and theaters throughout the South and Midwest; his work has also been featured on radio and television, and can be heard on numerous recordings, including the Tia Chucha Press poetry-music CD, "A Snake in the Heart." He currently serves on the Board of Directors of the Guild Complex.

Performance poet Marvin Tate is the author of *Schoolyard of Broken Dreams* (Tia Chucha Press). His poems, rants, chants, and all-out funklings have been heard on National Public Radio, The McNeil/Lehrer News Hour, and at Lollapalooza. His most recent CD with the word/theater/funk band, D-Settlement is called "The Minstrel Show." He is finishing his second book of poetry, *The Amazing Mr. Orange*.

Piri Thomas is the author of the classic book *Down These Mean Streets*, which has been in print for 31 years and is now available in Spanish translation, *Por Estas Calles Bravas*. He has two CDs of poetry and music, "Sounds of the Streets" and "No Mo' Barrio Blues." He is working on another documentary, *Every Child is Born a Poet* and travels extensively throughout the country, speaking at universities, schools, prisons, and in the community.

Quincy Troupe is the author of 12 books, including six volumes of poetry, the latest of which is *Choruses* (Coffee House Press). His forthcoming memoir of Miles Davis, *Miles and Me*, will be published in March 2000. He lives in La Jolla, California and teaches at the University of California in San Diego. He is the Editorial Director of the new magazine for men of color, *Code*.

Mark Turcotte lives in Fish Creek, Wisconsin, where he has been named a 1999 Literary Fellow by the Wisconsin Arts Board. He is author of three collections of poetry, with two new volumes on the way. His work is forthcoming in several journals, including *Poetry* and *Prairie Schooner*.

New York poet Frank Varela is the author of *Serpent Underfoot* (MARCH/Abrazo Press, 1993). His poetry has been published by *Revista Chicano-Riqueña, Another Chicago Magazine, The America's Review, Puerto del Sol*, and *The Bilingual Review*.

An NEA Fellow, Martha Modena Vertreace is a Distinguished Professor of English and poet-in-residence at Kennedy-King College, Chicago. Her most recent book is *Dragon Lady: Tsukimi* (Riverstone Press). Vertreace has won two Scottish Arts Council Grants (the first awarded to a writer who is not British), four Illinois Arts Council Literary Awards, an Illinois Arts Council Fellowship, and a Significant Illinois Poet Award, which Gwendolyn Brooks established.

Michael Warr served as Executive Director of the Guild Complex for the literary art center's first decade. His awards for poetry include a National Endowment for the Arts Fellowship and the Gwendolyn Brooks Significant Illinois Poet Award. He has been widely anthologized and is the author of the collection of poems *We Are All the Black Boy* (Tia Chucha Press).

Afaa Michael Weaver is a veteran of fifteen years as a blue-collar factory worker in his native Baltimore. Those fifteen years were his literary apprenticeship, and he holds a BA from Regents College and an MFA from Brown University. Afaa is the author of eight books of poetry, including *Talisman* (Tia Chucha Press). He is the Alumnae Professor of English at Simmons College in Boston, Massachusetts.

Larry Winfield has been an active, behind-the-scenes presence in the Chicago poetry community since 1990. He produces short films, edits and publishes *Liquid Glyph,* an on-line poetry magazine, leads an experimental group called Brass Orchid, and is the author of a poetry book, *Rosedust.* He helped give birth to the Guild Complex's National Poetry Video Festival.

About Guild Complex

Tia Chucha Press is the publishing wing of the Guild Complex, an award-winning, not-for-profit, literary arts center based in Chicago. The Complex serves as a forum for literary cross-cultural expression, discussion and education, in combination with other arts. We believe that the arts are instrumental in defining and exploring human experience, while encouraging participation by artists and audience alike in changing the conditions of our society. Through its culturally inclusive, primarily literary programming, the Guild Complex provides the vital link that connects communities, artists and ideas.

Guild Complex features weekly readings, performances, and open mics in Chicago. To become a member or donor, or for more information, contact our office at 773-296-1108 ext. 18 or by email at guildcomplex@earthlink.net.

Reviews and backlist of Tia Chucha Press books, as well the calendar of Complex events, conferences, and festivals, can be found on our website at http://nupress.nwu.edu/guild.